L.E.A.R.N.E.R.

Finding the True, Good, and Beautiful in Education

Marita Diffenbaugh

ConnectEDD Publishing

Chicago, Illinois

This publication is available at discount pricing when purchased in quantity for educational purposes, promotions, or fundraisers. For inquiries and details, contact the publisher at:
info@connecteddpublishing.com

Published by ConnectEDD Publishing LLC
Chicago, IL
www.connecteddpublishing.com

Cover Design: Kheila Dunkerly

L.E.A.R.N.E.R.: Finding the True, Good, and Beautiful in Education/ Marita Diffenbaugh. —1st ed.
Paperback ISBN: 978-1-7348908-6-0
Ebook ISBN: 978-1-7348908-7-7

Praise for *L.E.A.R.N.E.R.*

At a time when traditional classroom learning experiences have been profoundly disrupted by the COVID-19 pandemic, forcing students to learn via Zoom and reminding parents about the priceless value of great teachers, Marita Diffenbaugh's book is a timely and inspiring new manifesto for teachers everywhere. By putting the teacher-student relationship—teachers listening to the needs of students—back at the center of learning, she provides educators with a powerful tool to help them reclaim their sense of purpose and fulfill their critical mission.

—**Greg Carr,** Philanthropist. www.Gorongosa.org

Marita Diffenbaugh shines light on what is most important in education, people and relationships. This book comes to our world at an important time and takes us into the heart of learning: helping learners thrive by encouraging them in the true, good, and beautiful that they have to share. Strategies, resources, and encouragement throughout the chapters show us how, together, we can provide a service of education that matters now and will matter in the future.

—**Angela Maiers,** Founder, *Choose2Matter.* www.AngelaMaiers.com

A refreshing look at education in the 21st century, both what it is and what it could be. Diffenbaugh shows how to transform teaching from acts of doing **to** students and **for** students to a process of engaged presence in working **with** students.

—**Charles Elbot,** Co-author of *Building Intentional School Culture: Excellence in Academics and Character*, has served as a school principal for 22 years and has been a national leader in how to create an intentional school culture.

This book breaks down the components of a loving and supportive environment in which learners are prioritized and learning flourishes. While the book is focused on students, facilitating learning is itself a learning process for educators. The book lays out a simple and clear path to becoming a listening and empowering educator. Marita's writing is full of love and support for learners and educators. From the first day welcoming students to class to new ways of assessing student development, this book will prove a great guide for educators.

—**Louise Dubé,** iCivics Executive Director. www.iCivics.org

The science of learning has exploded over the last quarter century. Much of what we now know about the brain, how it develops and how children make sense of the world around them, too often collides with our current classroom practices and education policies. *L.E.A.R.N.E.R.* is written by a master educator for other classroom teachers. It shows what works for children and their learning by melding the professional and personal experiences, failures and successes of a 21st century classroom genius with the deepest understandings of human nature from our greatest thinkers like Plato.

—**Terry Ryan,** CEO of the education nonprofit Bluum, and co-author with John Abbott of *The Unfinished Revolution: Learning, Human Behavior, Community, and Political Paradox*

When I read a book about the teaching profession, I'm hoping for three things – to be validated, inspired, and challenged. I found all three in *L.E.A.R.N.E.R. Finding the True, Good, and Beautiful in Education.* Marita Diffenbaugh beautifully validates how teachers support learning in their spaces, inspires them to rethink all the facets of who a learner is and what a learner needs, and challenges them to activate new practices that will heighten this essential work teachers do on a daily basis.

—**Tammy McMorrow,** Teacher and author of *Gatekeepers: Let's Talk About Teaching*

Marita's passion for education, people, and children comes shining through. Filled with stories and practical ideas, Marita provides a wonderful pathway to joyful teaching for both new and experienced educators. Finding the true, good, and beautiful is what she has done her whole life and I'm grateful she has decided to share that with the world.

—**Dean Shareski,** Education Consultant and Strategist, Author of *Embracing a Culture of Joy*

I love this book! Educators are often advised to teach "the whole child," but rarely have I seen a resource as readable, comprehensive, and filled with classroom-tested strategies as I found in *L.E.A.R.N.E.R.* This rich compendium of common sense ideas reminds us there's so much more to teaching than pushing hundreds of standards out to students, and shows us how to bring back the wonder and joy of learning. This book is the best gift you could find for any teacher you care about.

—**Barbara Nemko, Ph.D.,** Napa County Superintendent of Schools

Marita provides a full-on look at the only way we can improve our education system: by focusing on LEARNING! With a clear style and ease of communicating ideas, Marita captures the reader's attention and keeps it from start to finish. The *Oath for Learners* is a great reminder that everything in our education system is about learning. There are learners and there is the facilitation of learning. She also captures the often missing piece that real learning occurs when the learner is engaged at a high level with material that challenges them and addresses their strengths and needs. An excellent read and useful tool.

—**David Cook,** Director of Innovation, Kentucky Department of Education

Marita has created a great resource for all "learners" in education, including principals, teachers, parents, and district leaders. It is obvious that Marita has poured herself and her wealth of personal experience into the book for our benefit. I would encourage people to read this work with an open mind. While most of the ideas included will not fall into the stereotypical box of traditional education, I believe Marita has captured much of the essential cultural shift that needs to occur to move education forward and accelerate meaningful learning at a personal level for students.

—**Dustin D. Barrett, Ph.D.,** Director of Curriculum and Instruction, West Ada School District

Ralph Waldo Emerson said, "Nothing great was ever achieved without enthusiasm." Marita Diffenbaugh has always led with enthusiasm and displayed a passion for life and learning. Through *L.E.A.R.N.E.R.,* Marita calls upon her vast experience, research, and love of learning to challenge learners at every level to believe we are capable of more. There are challenges in our education system and we can meet those challenges by focusing on the *True, Good, and Beautiful* opportunities for all learners.

—**David Roberts,** Technology Administrator, Boise School District

This book touched my parent heart, my teacher heart, and my community heart. It provides a clear pathway and rays of hope for all those who are rethinking what schools could — and should— be. Marita Diffenbaugh has put into words what so many of us are thinking. The way she weaves in her vast array of experiences as both a learner and a teacher makes this book SO good!

—**Theresa Carter,** Educator and Regional Support Specialist, Idaho Digital Learning Alliance

The COVID 19 Pandemic has accelerated the need to adapt or adopt new operating models for all organizations. Organizations/employers are dealing with rapid integration of technology, and innovation in policy and professional development. Schools are strained as they support needed changes in the responsibilities of students, parents, teachers, staff, administrators, and boards. Staying relevant in this rapidly changing world of work is critical. The author's pledge and understanding of the Socratic method of learning as described by his famous student Plato, is based on implementing these principles within the complete human being: their mind, body, heart, and spirit. Learners will find Marita Diffenbaugh's reference invaluable as a part of their personal reference library.

—**Doug Park,** Change Facilitator, Strategy Planner, and Leadership Coach

L.E.A.R.N.E.R. shares stories and resources through a tone that is easy to connect with and that readers are sure to fall in love with. Marita Diffenbaugh reminds us that we help learners grow from their mistakes when they are involved in the study of what has worked and hasn't worked in their learning.

—**Dacia Jones,** President, Expeditions in Education, www.expeditionsineducation.org

L.E.A.R.N.E.R. is incredibly insightful and inspirational. Diffenbaugh weaves a tapestry of ideas and research-based theories with her teaching and life experiences, connecting with the reader in a multitude of ways. Marita's personal and professional journey provide a powerful foundation on which she shares a wealth of practical tools, pedagogies, and ideas that will empower educators serving at all levels and subject areas. In a time when educators have more on their plates than ever before, Diffenbaugh focuses on some simple, yet powerful, concepts that will make a bigger impact on learning than any set of standards or benchmarks ever have.

—**Simon Miller,** Teacher, Coach, and Technology Director; Kellogg School District

Marita Diffenbaugh, a joyful learner herself, has captured the essence of what it means to be a learner. She weaves together the "true, good, and beautiful" of learning through personal examples from her own journey followed up with actionable next steps to apply L.E.A.R.N.E.R in your own educational context. Marita's depiction of what learning looks, feels, and sounds like exemplifies that we are ALL learners in a community together. If we take a moment to reflect, we can make beautiful learning moments that last long after they are completed. This book is a genuine difference maker.

—**Janet Avery,** EdS, Director of Curriculum, Jerome, ID

Dedication and Thanks

This book is dedicated to all who seek and share what is true, good, and beautiful.

Special thanks to all the difference makers in my life. You know who you are! Thank you for sharing your precious time to listen to my stories and for sharing yours with me. I'm grateful for the adventures that we have together. I love you and I love learning with you!

L.E.A.R.N.E.R.

Finding the True, Good, and Beautiful in Education

Marita Diffenbaugh

Table of Contents

CHAPTER 3

CHAPTER 4

CHAPTER 5

CHAPTER 6

L.E.A.R.N.E.R.

Introduction

An Oath for Learners

As a young mother, my need for advice quickly became apparent to my infant son's pediatrician. At the conclusion of his newborn check-up, she wrote her personal phone number on a slip of paper and handed it to me. Dr. Armour let me know that I could call her anytime I had questions and I often took her up on this offer. This was at a time before the Internet and *Ask-a-Nurse* hotlines had become part of a typical household, so Dr. Armour became my go-to resource for any sniffle, rash, cough, or fever that my little buddy experienced. Even when answering my calls in the middle of the night, she seemed happy to hear from me and offered suggestions in a caring and calm way.

During our second visit to the office, Dr. Armour handed me a piece of paper and a pen as she took my son in her arms to weigh and measure him. She asked me to write down all the things that I could do when my baby cried. I wrote down things like feeding, burping, changing, rocking, and singing. She looked at the paper and wrote down a few more items. Then she handed me my healthy little baby and the list and told me to keep it handy. Her advice felt prophetic, as my son soon developed colic and I put that list to use on the many long nights that followed. One night I couldn't console him with any of the items on the list, so I gave Dr. Armour a frantic call. Her kind and gentle response in the middle of the night was, "Where are you on the list?" I explained that I had gone through the list and nothing was helping. She then asked if I needed something to eat, a drink of water, or if I needed to use the restroom. I answered "yes" to all three questions. Dr. Armour gave me permission to put my crying baby down in a safe place, his crib, and then take care of my needs. She asked me to give her a call again in 5-10 minutes. Upon calling her back, my baby boy was still crying in my arms, yet I felt a sense of relief and calmness begin to set in. I asked her, "Now what can I do?" She kindly responded, "Start back at the top of the list." This was a turning point for me, as I realized that I had the skills and resources needed to care for my baby on my own.

Dr. Armour shared hope with me. She was an incredible mentor who not only taught me facts about how to care for my baby, she helped me learn how to care for myself. Until I could gain confidence in my own abilities, she was my hope in times of need. Dr. Armour helped me gain knowledge, skills, and confidence to care for a little life that was more precious to me than anything else in the world. This learning changed my thinking from being fearful when my baby cried to being able to problem solve and care for his needs with confidence. This personal experience made me realize that learning accelerates in times of need.

> learning accelerates in times of need
>
> ~

To help a learner, you need to be a learner and Dr. Armour made this a practice. She was a teacher, physician, and friend. She listened attentively and analyzed my situation. Then she helped me feel empowered by having me write my own list of stop-a-baby-from-crying strategies. She made it a point to know me and to understand the challenges that I faced as a teenage mother. She chose to be a resource and to personalize my care.

Doctors practice medicine with a common goal: for all their patients to improve or sustain their good health. Doctors study their patients, looking for symptoms, needs, and patterns and then provide treatment accordingly. When you hear someone say that a doctor has a "good bedside manner," they are referring, in large part, to how well a doctor listens to a patient.

One of the oldest binding documents in history is the Hippocratic Oath. The principles traditionally attributed to Hippocrates, a Greek Physician from the 4th Century, are still held sacred by physicians today. Across the centuries, the Hippocratic Oath has served as a timeless agreement concerning a physician's conduct: they are to treat the sick to the best of their ability, preserve patient privacy, and teach the secrets of medicine to the next generation.

Think about your last medical appointment. Was there a **listening** exchange between you and the medical team that helped you? Did you feel **empowered**? What information was **analyzed**? Were you offered **resources** that supported your **needs**? How was your overall **experience**? Do you feel like you have a trusting **relationship** with your medical care provider? You might recognize some of these questions from surveys that you've been asked to take after a medical visit. If your medical care provider is incorporating these steps, then you will feel safe, supported, and have a plan. Isn't this what we hope for our children when they go to school?

In addition to health and safety, we hope that our schools provide a place for students to cultivate positive relationships and learn valuable skills and knowledge. There is power in the verb, "learn." If we think of learning in the same way we think of health, learning becomes a lifestyle, not merely a destination. As new information is available and personal needs evolve, we change, update, and continue to learn. When I studied to become a teacher, I had one goal in mind that I still carry with me today. I wanted to be there for others in their moments of learning. When wonder meets an understanding, when prediction gets tested through an experiment, and when you see the joy and sense of accomplishment in the eyes of another human, you know it. A commonality among many educators is the feeling of fulfillment when they see the "WOW" factor occur in a learner. This draws them to the profession.

Now, twenty-plus years later, I have experienced many shifts in my approach to learning and learners. I've used a variety of curriculum resources and instructional strategies. Some resources were purchased by my employer(s) and we were required to use these "with fidelity," as they promised to be the answer to help all students learn. The definition of fidelity is described as "faithfulness to a person, cause, or belief, demonstrated by continuing loyalty and support." As teachers, if our loyalty is based solely on the facilitation of curriculum or support for the content, we risk not seeing students' needs and being responsive to them. Think of a time when you've noticed allegiance to something such as a resource, strategy, or schedule versus the learner you were trying to support.

I'm thinking of a teacher who cried during professional development, when she was given permission to create lessons in response to her learners, rather than following the curriculum pacing guide. Her tears came from the realization that she had lost something when her district shifted to a practice of having all teachers offering the same lessons at the same time. She remembered her early years of teaching, when she had the flexibility to focus on the growth of the learner and she made a decision that day to bring that kind of reflective and responsive teaching back to her students.

I've empathized with a frustrated educator as they explained their reasons for wanting to remove all technology use from their students because a few students were being inappropriate with their use of Chromebooks. The comment shared was, "I did fine without using technology when I was in school." What served us well in the 20th Century, might not be fine in the 21st Century. Technology has changed the way we communicate, the way we conduct business, and the way that we learn. Integrating technology into our instructional design should enhance efforts to support our students' learning needs.

As information, resources, policies, and practices change at a rapid pace, how could a timeless guide serve educators, one that could be valuable and honored, much like the Hippocratic Oath has been for physicians? How might this guide help ensure that, as educators, we will keep our focus on the learner in efforts to support their learning growth? A Code of Ethics for professional educators is provided through licensing and certification processes; however, there is currently no common oath for the profession of teaching. What we do have is a lot of information to sort through: The what, the how, the when, the where, and the who, along with pedagogy, standards, curriculum, grading, social-emotional support, personalized learning, mastery-based, restorative practices, safety protocols, and much more. Just like doctors, we have ever-changing information, high expectations for care, support, and progress. Educators spend a lot of time sorting through important information, resources, and experiences to use upon need or request.

In preparation for this book, I have reflected on my childhood memories, along with my teaching, coaching, leadership, and parenting experiences, looking to answer two critical questions:

1. What is learning?
2. What do learners need?

I looked for common themes and messages through my curation of notes, tweets, blog posts, bookmarks, and even some sketch notes. I unpacked conversations, books, and inspirational movies in which teachers not only helped their students, but also transformed themselves in the process. After much reflection, I found some treasure. I put the treasure to a test by dreaming a bit and asking myself this question, "If I were to start a school from scratch, what would I look for when hiring amazing people who would be serving our students?" I would search for those who are willing to partner with a learner, to listen and look, to view the world through the learner's eyes and see what they hold as true, good, and beautiful. If every individual on a school team truly knows the people they serve, then they are on the right track for discovering what is valued and needed to encourage learning.

The following acronym will be easy to remember because it spells the word **LEARNER** and is where the treasure I discovered is stored. This acronym can be used as a tool to help teachers sort content, processes, and tools in order to ensure that relevant and responsive learning opportunities are available for all learners. It is my hope that you allow yourself some time for reflective thinking in between the seven chapters of this book. To help you in this process, I've included some questions, activities, or resources at the end of each chapter. The treasure that I'm sharing is for teachers, and that includes you. Whether you carry that title or not, we are all teachers. Take time to reflect on your own stories that you think about when you read this book. As you read, you might find areas that you'd like to improve upon; please give yourself grace when you discover something that you'd like to change about yourself. If this happens, just take on the job of a learner and grow. Thank you for being here, this book is for you.

Listen, **E**mpower, **A**nalyze, **R**esources, **N**eeds, **E**xperiences, **R**elationships

The ***L.E.A.R.N.E.R.*** acronym can be turned into an *Oath for Learners,* that we, as educators, can pledge to our students:

> As a teacher, I pledge to **listen** to and **empower** my students to develop their full potential. I will **analyze** and study my students. I will help provide hope to my students by matching **resources** to their **needs** and providing **experiences** that support each student's growth. I will model the power of a team

and help my students build lasting **relationships.** Ultimately, I realize that to help a learner, I need to be a learner myself.

This *Oath for Learners* is versatile and can be personalized for any role or relationship that seeks to support learning and can be customized for a specific learner. Fill in the blanks, as you'd like for administrators, parents, friends, grandparents, community members, students, etc.

As a __________, I pledge to **listen** to and **empower** _________ to develop his/her full potential. I will **analyze** and study __________. I will help provide hope to _________ by matching **resources** to his/her **needs** and provide **experiences** that support his/her growth. I will model the power of a team and help _________build lasting **relationships.** Ultimately, I realize that to help a learner, I need to be a learner myself.

The *Oath for Learners* can be used as a guide to have ongoing conversations about what learning looks like and sounds like in your district, school, and home. How do we know when learning is happening?

When hope is present, then learning is possible for anyone. Never give up on a learner. We can take from Dr. Armour's baby-crying strategy and apply it to our Response to Intervention (RTI) practices or student data meetings. Have lists of strategies, resources, and activities that have worked for helping students learn. Start on the lists and try one thing at a time, observe and record what works and what doesn't. If you get the bottom of the lists and nothing has worked for a student that you are trying to reach, pause. Check on yourself and care for any needs that you might have. Are you hungry? Do you need a break? When is the last time that you had a proper belly laugh? After pausing, head back to the list and try again. What didn't work today, might just work tomorrow, or the next day. You can be a hope giver by helping your students find the true, good, and beautiful in their educational journey.

True, Good, and Beautiful

I had the opportunity to meet an incredible hope giver, while sitting next to him on a plane. Throughout the flight, we swapped stories about how we've been inspired to learn and how we've helped learners throughout our careers. After the plane landed, Charles Elbot handed me a gift of his book, *Building an Intentional School Culture.* In the book, Elbot and his co-author Fulton (2008) share a connection between education and Plato's three ways of knowing: the True, Good, and Beautiful:

> *"Plato's three ways of knowing offer a helpful perspective on school culture in the education of young people. Plato described the first way of knowing as True. The True is what most of our academic standards focus on, academic content and skills...The second way of knowing is the Good. This is about being virtuous: about not only identifying with "me" but also with "we." It is about empathy, service to others, good citizenship, and character education...The third way of knowing is the Beautiful, which is about spirit, presence, poetry, and artistic sensibility...a school culture can be designed deliberately to hold each of these three ways of knowing and foster ways for all three to resonate with each other so our young people can build flourishing lives, contribute to their communities, and be of benefit to the generations who follow them."*
> *(Building an Intentional School Culture: Excellence in Academics and Character* Charles Elbot, David Fulton, 2008, viii).

Plato's *True, Good, and Beautiful* referenced in Elbot and Fulton's work is echoed within Daniel Pink's research on what motivates humans. In his book, *Drive* (2009), he describes three essential elements of motivation: Mastery, Purpose, and Autonomy. In Pink's work, *mastery* is a desire to continuously improve at something that matters. This connects to the "True" in education, as K-12 content standards are meant to help prepare students for something that matters in their future. When Pink refers to *purpose*, he explains how this is a wish to be a part of something larger than ourselves. *Purpose* corresponds to the "Good" that happens in school, when learners are engaging in teamwork, collaboration, community service, and character-building. The "Beautiful" in education is when learners can create or experience something that is appealing, or even delightful, to them. "Beautiful" aligns to Pink's *autonomy*, which incorporates the need for choice in our learning and the desire to lead our own lives.

Our values, beliefs, and experiences help frame what we believe to be true, good, and beautiful. Schools and districts have core values, guiding principles, and mission or vision statements to communicate the shared agreements or overarching goals for serving their students.

Does the information that we use to measure our success help us find what is true, good, and beautiful about education? How does the data we collect help us understand who students are, where they've been, and what their future goals might be?

The *Oath for Learners* will help us sort the data, content, processes, and tools we use to ensure that learning happens for each student that we serve. Each chapter in this book takes an in depth look at each word in the L.E.A.R.N.E.R. acronym, identifying key components of the word, why it matters, and how we can best address it in our classrooms and schools. Throughout each chapter, look for the true, good, and beautiful, for when all three of these are present, we can be sure that we are thorough in honoring and supporting our learners, as whole people.

CHAPTER 1

Listen: Where is Your Attention?

Listen, *Empower, Analyze, Resources, Needs, Experiences, Relationships*

"The beginning is the most important work."
Plato

Learning begins with listening. Listening to determine a need, hearing about a challenge, and looking for ways that we can gain new knowledge to support something we believe to be valuable. The *Oath for Learners* starts with **Listen** because this is the beginning step and a fundamental requirement when supporting learners in the process of learning.

Our education system can learn a lot from how great teachers listen to their students. Great teachers listen to determine if the learning is relevant to the learner by ensuring that the content, processes, and tools are **true** connections that will be helpful to them in the world. Great teachers help learners see how they can use their learning to support others and listen for ways to help students share **good** in their community. Great teachers listen and look for learners' readiness to create, jump into action, and take **beautiful** risks to share their learning with others.

Miss Williams, my sixth-grade teacher, was one of these great teachers. She knew me. She knew what I was interested in, what I was really good at, and what I struggled with. Her classroom was active and filled with surprises, from art projects, science experiments, and math challenges, to our unique classroom pets: two boa constrictors. There was a harmony that took place, a balance between learner-centered and teacher-directed activities that would make the day fly by. In fact, we would groan when the bell rang for us to go home.

Miss Williams gave us the opportunity to work as a team when she experienced a health challenge half-way through the year. She wrote us letters that arrived at our homes to explain that she would be out of school for a procedure, and when she returned we would adapt to her not having a voice to use for a while. We were so happy when Miss Williams returned to school, we all wanted to help her, and we worked especially hard to get along. The way that she invited us to be part of helping solve the challenge was vulnerable on her part, but this helped our class grow and take on new responsibilities. She treated us like members of a team, giving us the gift of high expectations, and believing in us to meet them. Miss Williams helped me find my strengths and encouraged me to share them with others.

Effective listening starts with observation. Impactful teachers study their students by looking and listening for ways to support learning and growth. They help students recognize when learning is happening by pausing to observe what learning looks like, sounds like, and feels like.

Finding True Learning Connections

What keeps teachers from listening and responding to their students' learning needs? For some, this could be the required curriculum and standards that have been scheduled on calendars and within grade levels. When I was teaching, I felt a constant push to get all students through the required curriculum and standards, within the allotted time, regardless of learner readiness. For some students, the required expectation would not be attainable, until they had learned prerequisite skills. For example, to understand how multiplication works, a learner needs to have number sense and understand the concept of addition. Learning maps or curriculum documents that list a continuum of content and skills are needed guides; however, they must adjust to learners' needs. Expecting all students to be at the same place and at the same time can deter teachers from listening to their students and hinder them from making true learning connections.

One of the most difficult things to navigate in education are the hundreds, or even thousands, of required K-12 content standards. In order to find true learning connections, we need to first listen for the relevance within learning requirements. With this information, we can help students see the value of the expectation by listening for ways to connect to their current interests and strengths. For especially powerful connections, we can listen in our communities and in our world to help students see how the learning expectation will be an asset to them in the future. Finally, we can look at the learning expectation and make sure that the learner has the capacity to take this on by considering their learning workload of other expectations that they are currently being asked to achieve.

Are all required K-12 standards relevant for all learners? Throughout my diverse roles from the classroom to the state department, I've discovered that many learning requirements are expecting students to become experts in too many areas. When students are overloaded, they can become overwhelmed or apathetic. Providing students with meaningful and achievable learning targets will help them find true learning connections that matter to them. We are fortunate to have information and expertise at our fingertips through the technology that we use every day. Consider how technology has changed the way that you ask for help when you have challenges at your home or your work. Do our K-12 content standards take into consideration the resources that our students have at their fingertips?

A recommendation shared through an Educational Leadership article (2001) "How and Why Standards Can Improve Student Achievement: A Conversation with Robert J. Marzano," offered a solution to "Cut the number of standards and content within standards dramatically. If you look at all the national and state documents that McREL has organized on its Web site (www.mcrel.org), you'll find approximately 130 across some 14 different subject areas. The knowledge and skills that these documents describe represent about 3,500 benchmarks. To cover all of this content, you would have to change schooling from K-12 to K-22" (p. 14).

As I write this, we are nineteen years past the above conversation, in which Marzano (2001) recommended reducing standards by two-thirds. Are we listening to education experts, our students, and our communities to ensure that what we teach and pay attention to are relevant and true learning connections? The good news is that many communities are sorting through and highlighting the essential standards that are relevant today, and, in turn, are implementing those that help students become lifelong learners and contributors in the future.

The Coronavirus pandemic has created a virtual connection between home and school like never before. Through video conferences, email threads, and phone conversations, there are opportunities to listen for relevance and offer true learning connections that are valuable to our students, their families, and our communities. From the home, to the in-person or virtual classroom, to the boardroom, people are reflecting on what is most important for students to know and be able to do and what resources and support will encourage continual learning.

In a sense, we have been forced to "clean the garage" together and it is the first time in my education career that I've experienced so much agreement as to what the essentials are for student learning. I have heard some common themes that are powerful human qualities, and that align with the Six Global Competencies for Deep Learning: Character, Citizenship, Collaboration, Communication, Creativity, and Critical Thinking, (Fullan, M., Quinn, J., & McEachen, J. (2018).

Think of your garage or a closet that is in need of attention. I'm thinking of my garage that continues to accumulate items. My husband and I will set a time to organize the garage; it is an event. We usually sort by four categories, what we use all the time, what we use seasonally/sometimes, what we hope to use, and what we are not using. The last two categories take time, requiring us to engage in conversation, list pros/cons, and, ultimately, arrive at a consensus. How does our education system "clean the garage" to ensure that all standards are essential and relevant? How are standards created or reviewed? When teachers and students have clear and achievable targets, they can focus their time, resources, and feedback to teaching and learning these. When you are ready to "clean the garage" at your school, district, or state, do this in response to what you know about your students, your community, and the world at the time. When districts and schools are diligent about ensuring that learning essentials/standards/goals are relevant today while forecasting what is needed for the future, this gives teachers the flexibility to help learners make true learning connections.

Sharing the Good

Our family was sitting around the campfire one summer evening, looking for shooting stars, telling stories, and building s'mores, when we heard some coyotes singing in the distance. My four-year-old granddaughter's eyes widened as she asked, "Are coyotes good?" We assured her that we were safe and that coyotes were just talking to each other, like we were at the campfire. Her word choice, "good" helped me understand that she connects this word to being nice, safe, and acceptable.

Who determines what is good? You do, people do, our community as a whole does. During times of crisis, you can hear goodness through the challenge and turmoil. People rise up to be there for each other. During the COVID-19 pandemic, there has been a steady beat of goodness shared throughout the world. Music has been a universal language playing through social media posts such as a spontaneous balcony duet in Barcelona, featuring Celine Dion's "My Heart Will Go On," shared between a pianist and a saxophone player. An Italian neighborhood chorus of Chris Tomlin's "How Great is Our God," and a school choir in the United States, sharing their concert through video, each chiming in from their homes to brighten the world with "Somewhere Over the Rainbow." Doorbells have been ringing bringing hope through a meal, needed household supplies, or hands-on school activities. In times of difficulty people come together, and this is good.

What does it mean to be a good person, good worker, and good citizen? Harvard Graduate School of Education hosts, "The Good Project," (2020) an investigation of how professionals do good work through 3 E's of "Excellent, Engaging, and Ethical." If you check out their resources online, be sure to look for the Value Sort Activity, which can be used to help an individual determine what their core values are. Have you listened to the core values that your students, families, and colleagues have? Have you shared yours?

Helping students find ways to contribute, not only makes a difference to others, it creates authentic learning opportunities for them. Service learning is a way to provide students with experiences that support the greater good. These experiences are especially powerful when students are directing them. There was a time when one of my students wanted to provide help for a community that had suffered due to a tsunami. This student shared facts about the needs this community had and then came up with a plan of how our school could help by conducting a penny drive. The pennies added up to a good sum to send to families in need that lived in the community impacted by the tsunami.

Helping students realize that they are a vital part of a community and can make a difference locally, nationally, or globally while providing them with an opportunity to be a contributing citizen. Justice Sandra Day O'Connor, along with her iCivics team has reimagined civic education by offering a powerful legacy gift to students and teachers through iCivics.org. O'Connor's iCivics team is using the way that students like to play through gaming to create simulations and games that will help them learn how to become contributing citizens in their communities. A feature of iCivics helps students collect Impact Points as they play and these can be spent on the featured Impact Projects. Impact projects support a variety of needs from pediatric cancer research to providing books to young learners, and much more. iCivics has found a win-win with this educational resource that helps encourage positive citizenship, while connecting those in need to people who have ways to help.

How does your school or district reach out to others to truly listen for ways to make a difference? Service learning, teaching about how to be a contributing citizen through civic education, and caring for those in need with random acts of kindness are some ways to help students share goodness with others.

Give some #DifferenceMaker Shout-Outs. Celebrate those making a difference by sharing the good that happens in your classroom or school through newsletters, notes, or social media venues. Consider taking a few minutes to write a handwritten note or give a virtual shout out to someone who has shared some good and contributed to be a difference maker for others. Listening and responding to a need by sharing goodness is something to highlight and curate, as this creates a ripple effect and others hearing your stories will look for ways to be difference makers, too.

Taking Beautiful Risks

Listen and look for learner readiness. When students have reasons for learning and an authentic audience to share their learning with, then they are ready to take a beautiful risk. Beautiful risks incorporate opportunities to use their creativity, to take action, and to accept a challenge.

Creating safe learning environments for taking beautiful risks by trying something new—even though it might not work out—takes courage and support. Mistakes are lessons and are part of the learning process. Ronald Beghetto's ASCD publication (2018) "Taking Beautiful Risks in Education," highlights three strategies schools can adopt to ensure that creativity is part of learning:

1. Rethink the formula for school success
2. Share Favorite Failures
3. Building an Unshakeable Sense of Possibility Thinking

Beghetto explains how "A beautiful risk involves taking actions that have the potential to make a positive and lasting contribution to the learning and lives of others. A child who leaves the safety of a popular peer group to stand with a kid who is isolated or being picked on is taking a beautiful risk" (2018, p.18).

New learning experiences can feel scary. A recent hiking adventure put me into the shoes of a learner who is feeling like they're on a ledge and ready to fall or fail, right in front of their friends. My husband and I felt ready to hike Mt. Borah, the highest mountain in Idaho, as we had been practicing other elevation hikes and were excited for the next level challenge. We had listened to the warnings to be cautious at all times and to pack enough water. We started early in the morning with only a narrow beam of light to guide us and our senses were on high alert. Watching a couple of animal hikers, a mother and baby Bighorn Sheep, barrel down a steep grade with ease, made us feel even more unprepared for our next steps, which we thought was the exposed knife-edge ridge known as Chicken Out Ridge. As the sun came up, we were scaling the side of a mountain with tiny edges to grab with our hands and feet. At one point, my husband helped me stretch my arm to reach a handhold and I looked down realizing that this was more risk that we had bargained for. Each movement was done with care and prayer and finally, we climbed to an opening and celebrated yelling, "We didn't chicken-out! We did it!" Another hiker came from the other side of the mountain, and said, "That wasn't Chicken Out Ridge; that is!" and he pointed to the craggy mountain top just ahead of us. The part of the mountain that we accidentally climbed ended up being more challenging to us than Chicken Out Ridge, as it was more like a free solo rock-climbing adventure. When we made it to the summit of Mt. Borah—12,662 feet in elevation, we were elated. The promise of the summit views and the powerful feeling that comes from reaching our goal, is what keeps us on the hook for climbing more mountains. Every mountain top experience provides us with lessons to learn.

Learners are risk-takers; they allow courage and curiosity to be louder than doubt and fear.

Learners are risk-takers; they allow courage and curiosity to be louder than doubt and fear. When is the last time you created something and then shared it? As I'm writing this book, I'm letting my courage be louder than my fear of sharing thoughts in such a permanent way. If only this book could be shared as a live Google document, where I could revise as I learn and experience more.

What makes doubt or fear so loud? We have given a lot of power to the letter F, and the word "Fail." When this word connects to the value of the person, rather than it being just a way to communicate feedback of what has been learned, it damages. Think back to an epic failure that left you nervous about putting yourself out there again. One of my epic failures took place at our state Capitol building during a professional development event that hosted about 1,500 teachers throughout the course of two days. At the time, I served in a district as an Instructional Technology Manager and was launching cloud-based computing and K-12 educational resources. The first group of teachers arrived with their own devices and we had a great session. The second group of teachers came later that morning, and about half of them were unable to access WIFI. This was frustrating to some; however, we gimped along by having them share a device with a partner. When the last group came in the afternoon, no one was able to connect to the Internet, even though we were frantically trying to troubleshoot and help them. This third group left frustrated and feeling like their time would have been better used somewhere else. We found out later that there was a WIFI setting for the building allowing only a certain number of users to connect within a 24-hour period. This happened to be the first time that many users tried to use the Internet at the same time at our Capitol Building.

This was a difficult failure to recover from, but I came up with a plan to make amends. I scheduled a visit with each school in our district to provide a Digital Citizenship presentation, and I brought every teacher a red folder, labeled Plan B: Help and Resources, with a quote from Victor Hugo, "Perseverance, a secret of all triumphs." The red folder could be used to hold a ready-to-go activity for when technology would let them down.

What would be in your red folder with a ready-to-go strategy, the next time that you experience failure? I hope that grace is front and center, as failing is part of learning, not something to fear or feel ashamed of. The book, *Gift of Failure,* (2015) by Jessica Lahey offers perspective about failure and why so many learners are afraid to fail. Lahey explains how we all come equipped with curiosity, and therefore, come into this world motivated to learn and explore. If students are lacking engagement in school and not accessing their natural abilities of curiosity on a regular basis, we need to evaluate how our district, school, or classroom encourages beautiful risks in learning. What we celebrate shines light on what a learning community thinks is valuable and important.

Dean Shareski explains in his book, *Embracing a Culture of Joy*: "In a world that needs innovators, creators, and problem solvers, we may be focusing on the wrong things. Yet we tend to celebrate students based on grades and award ceremonies that remain focused on numbers. We should focus on something better—the love of learning" (2017, p. 14). Take a quick inventory of all celebrations provided by your school or district. Do these celebrate the love of learning?

Activate LISTEN for Learners

At the start of this chapter, we started with Plato's quote, "The beginning is the most important work" and asked the question, "Where is Your Attention?" We discovered the importance of listening for <u>relevance</u> in what we are teaching our students, listening for ways that students can <u>contribute</u> in their community, and listening for students' <u>readiness</u> to create, share, and take action with their knowledge and skills. Listening is the important first step in helping learners make true learning connections (relevance), share the good (contribution), and take beautiful risks (readiness) that will help them reach their goals, help them to grow, and make a difference in their lives and in the lives of others.

Finding True Learning Connections: What is essential for K-12 students to learn? When answering this, get a diverse team together to help "clean the garage." Involve students/families/business owners/community members and have an ongoing process to review K-12 learning essentials. Follow the students throughout their K-12 career. Are the required standards/learning essentials making a difference throughout K-12, after 2nd grade, 4th grade, 6th grade, 9th grade, 12th grade, or after high school? How is the workload for students at each step of the journey; are we asking too much? Not enough? What are we hearing about what is essential when we listen to our students?

Share the Good: How does your school or classroom highlight the good that students are a part of? In addition to highlighting through thank you notes and social media posts, consider offering a regular Community Listening Post event. The purpose of these events is to provide an opportunity for parents, community members, students, staff and other interested parties to listen to learning stories and learning needs. This is a great place to celebrate learning! Have the listening go both ways by inviting community members to share their ideas for education. This valuable exchange will help to align educational goals with the needs in the workforce.

Taking Beautiful Risks: How is your district or school modeling learning? Educators can create and display their own learning plans for students to see. Learning is cultivated in others when they see people they admire putting themselves out there as learners and sharing their successes and failures. Celebrate the learning process and let students see you encourage your colleagues in their learning, as well. Invite learners to share their learning plans and goals with others. Offering opportunities for learners to create, share, and take action helps build a culture that listens for, expects, and honors learning.

Finding the True, Good, and Beautiful

This chapter provides opportunities to look at the *True,* through learning connections; the *Good*, through difference making; and the *Beautiful,* through taking risks to share creativity. As you continue reading the chapters that follow, bring the True, Good, and Beautiful with you. Take a look at the following table to see how this can be used as a sorting tool, when learning new things, reflecting on your practice, or *listening* to your students and helping them understand the value of their learning goals.

True	Good	Beautiful
Academic Content	Team	Wonder/ Phenomenon
Facts	Workforce "Life Skills"	Creativity
Essential Competencies/ Standards	Connections/ Collaboration	Strengths/Interests
Knowledge	**Skills**	**Dispositions/ Character**
I Know...	So That I Can...	Which Helps Me...

CHAPTER 2

Empower: Who is Learning?

Listen, ***Empower,*** *Analyze, Resources, Needs, Experiences, Relationships*

"Do not train a child to learn by force or harshness; but direct them to it by what amuses their minds, so that you may better be able to discover with accuracy the peculiar bent of the genius of each."

Plato

This chapter is dedicated to exploring ways that we can empower the learners in our lives. A place to begin is with empathy, the way in which we put ourselves in someone else's shoes. In our *Oath for Learners*, we started with **Listen** and by doing that we've collected some important information. As we discover what inspires learners, we can **Empower** them. Empowering students comes easily when we believe that every person has what Plato refers to in the above quote, "a peculiar bent of genius." Empowering learners begins with the way that we see them and welcome them into our learning community.

Some learners come to school already aware of their value and how they can use their talents and strengths to contribute; some students need help in discovering their awesomeness.

Welcome, This is a Good Place for You!

Instead of asking "Are students ready for school?" let's ask "Is school ready for students?" When learners begin school with an assessment, such as a kindergarten orientation or grade level test, we might be jumping ahead. Before analyzing academic strengths and weaknesses, parents and kids are hoping to hear, "We see you, you belong here, and we will help you grow from here." To measure how we are doing with our school welcome message, let's look at a welcome that we hope our students had when they joined us in this world.

Family and friends experience indescribable and immediate love when a new baby is born. There is a shared understanding that this new little life is dependent upon them to care for their comfort, development, safety, and all their needs. There is a shared hope for this new little human to be surrounded by what is true, good, and beautiful from this moment on. Fast forward five years, and this little one arrives at school for the first day of kindergarten to begin their K-12 learning adventure. From the first day of school to high school graduation, learners of all ages need to be listened to, empowered, and loved.

Are we ready to love each elementary, middle, or high school student who walks into our classroom or school? Not only do kids deserve this, love is what will truly help them flourish. Kids learn because they are curious, and they come to school to play with their friends and meet you. Ask your students or children what their best part of school is and you might find some connections to Plato's ways of knowing. My granddaughter didn't hesitate when telling me about her best part of preschool in this order, "being rowdy with my friends" (good), "learning my letters" (true), and "making things" (beautiful). When students have a difficult time thinking about what is best about school, chances are they are not feeling listened to or empowered.

My student-teaching ended in middle school, and my teaching career began in kindergarten. After developing strategies to empower and support middle schoolers in their learning, I remember thinking how vast this grade level jump would be and prepared myself for a whole new experience. I was surprised to discover that many of the strategies that worked well for middle school students were also effective for young learners. Learners are learners; while the content and skill level changes, the process of learning is the same. Learners of all ages need to see how the learning goals or expectations help them in some way or connect to something that they are interested in learning about. Like sixth graders, these kindergartners were discovering who they were and deciding who their friends would be. Middle school students taught me that a welcome to school should not be a list of rules and procedures. Before making requests and establishing expectations, offer activities for students to get to know you and each other. I think this is an area that needs improvement in school. How many first days are filled with procedures, rules, and conversations about what students shouldn't be doing? How many first days of the week start this way? Why are Fridays sometimes better than Mondays?

At any grade level, the welcome to school should start with activities that let students know that their presence matters and that they are safe to learn. Have you heard someone say, "All eyes on me" in a classroom? Teachers use this phrase to ensure that they are being listened to when giving instruction, and when students are giving their full attention this can feel empowering. Learners can benefit from the same kind of experience, where they are being looked at and listened to as they share a question or explain something.

Activities that help students share their strengths, interests, and needs are essential to building a culture of learning. On the first day of kindergarten, after giving students a tour around their classroom and school, they were offered a variety of activities such as listening to stories, drawing a picture using their favorite color crayon, and sharing about something fun that they did during the summer. I kept a notebook handy to write down observations and check off levels of ability that I noticed from the students' participation. I looked for how each student interacted during their station choices. Were they able to choose an activity and follow through with it? Did they work alone or with a peer? Did they wander to other places in the room and not connect with the activities? I redirected students only for safety reasons, and spent less time talking and more time watching and listening. Offering students opportunities to learn without step-by-step or follow-the-teacher instruction will show teachers how their students prefer to learn and where they can use support.

How do we empower students who are hurting? About two weeks into school, I learned that a new student would be joining our class who had recently experienced the tragic loss of his mother. When I met Tyson, I recognized my own pain and hurt in his eyes, as I had just lost my dad earlier in the year to cancer. Tyson didn't talk very much. He didn't want to play or try any of the learning activities; he just quietly cried. I made a special place for him near my desk where he could sit with pillows and books and cry anytime he needed to. I let him know that at recess, if he wanted to have a friend, I'd join him and cry, too. I would cry about missing my dad and he would cry about missing his mom. I let him know that when he wanted to have a break from crying, he could play and join the learning activities. Over time, Tyson cried less and played and participated in activities more. Soon, he was drawing pictures and writing stories about his mom and his family. At this time, I had not received any formal training on how to help a student who had experienced trauma; however, I was able to share hope with Tyson because I knew what he was going through. Tyson and I shared the way of knowing that Plato refers to as the "**Good**," identifying what we had in common and sharing empathy and care in a time of need.

Empowering someone who is hurting can start with empathy and should be followed up with resources and support to help them in their healing.

In addition to seeing hurt through tears, you might also hear hurt sound vulgar and see it act tough. A group of pre-teens at our school had a reputation for causing trouble during lunch break. I had observed their habits and the consequences that they earned for a couple of weeks. Then I invited them into my classroom for a special lunch. I told them that they could bring their hot lunch or sack lunch and I would supply dessert.

In addition to seeing hurt through tears, you might also hear hurt sound vulgar and see it act tough.

All seven of my students showed up and looked at each other inquisitively as they saw me sitting at a table that had a tablecloth, folded napkins, silverware, plates, and slices of chocolate cake waiting for each of them. As they ate their lunch, we talked about anything that they wanted to talk about, video games, camping, football. Then I explained that I had an important mission for them, if they chose to accept it, that would involve a lunch like this every month. On the other days, they would be participating in this mission on the playground. "What is it, Mrs. D.?" the leader of the group asked. Yes! I knew that I had hooked them.

"Well, there are some students who are not feeling safe and respected on the playground. We need to find out what is causing this and then brainstorm ways to help resolve it."

We set up expectations of how they would collect this data and what playground duty to report to daily with the information. Then I explained that on the last Friday of each month, I'd bring dessert and they could bring their hot lunch or sack lunch to join me and we would talk about their progress. We called it "Mission Impossible" and it worked. These kids needed a fresh start, and by giving them positive attention and an important job to do, they were able to reset.

A mentor of mine once explained that whatever is happening in the world will eventually make its way across the doorstep of the school. This means that our kids will come with good and with bad, and we need to be prepared to help them with both extremes and everything in between.

Learners are the customers that schools support. It's all about the learner. Without learners, there would be no school. Angela Maiers' *The You MATTER Manifesto* (2011) incorporates powerful words that can challenge us to welcome each person by remembering their value. Think about a student who has been the most difficult to work and learn with lately, and put their name in place of "You" in the following:

<u>The You MATTER Manifesto</u>
You are enough
You have influence
You have a contribution to make
You have a gift that others need
Your actions define your impact
You are the change
You matter
(Angela Maiers, 2011)

How students are welcomed to school each day influences how they will choose to participate. Teachers who empower their students by offering authentic compliments and providing supportive feedback are opening the door for learning to happen.

100% Human

Children of all ages are 100% human. From the beginning of life to the end of life, we all have at least one thing in common, each one of us is

100% human. Do we see each child as a whole person? Are students empowered in the same way that adults would be if they were enrolled in your school?

While we are all 100% human, there is no human that is exactly the same as another. We have diverse strengths and weaknesses, along with variety in culture, beliefs, and experiences. All humans can learn; however, there may be barriers to a student's learning and it is up to educators, leaders, and parents to meet learners where they are and support their continued growth. Some learning barriers come from lack of essential human needs. "You can't Bloom until you Maslow" is a common phrase shared in education circles. *Maslow's Hierarchy of Needs* (1943) are listed from the bottom of the hierarchy upward to include: physiological, safety, love and belonging, esteem, and self-actualization. In order for a person to access the learning that Bloom's Taxonomy (1956) refers to in six levels (knowledge, comprehension, application, analysis, synthesis, and evaluation) from basic understanding to mastery, we must care for essential human needs.

A learning barrier arises when a student does not see the value in a learning expectation. Helping students connect their interests to goals and expectations results in them taking ownership of their learning and removes this barrier. In my early years of teaching, I used to ask students what they wanted to be when they grew up. I've since changed my question to inquire more about what students enjoy doing or what they are curious about. Instead of having an occupation or job title motivate students, let's empower them to honor their unique strengths and interests.

Instead of having an occupation or job title motivate students, let's empower them to honor their unique strengths and interests.

Schools are not alone in shifting the question from "What do you want to be?" to "Who are you?" Check out the top three of 125 Common Interview Questions (2020), from Indeed.com:

1. Tell me about yourself.
2. How would you describe yourself?
3. What makes you unique?

I've personally experienced two interview questions that still have me thinking. Answering these questions provided a window into my thinking, my experiences, and my beliefs about myself:

- Tell us five words that best describe who you are.
- You have one minute to tell us everything that you can do with a brick.

These are not easy questions to answer. There is not one right answer. These responses require self-awareness, confidence, and metacognition.

Who inspired you in your career path? While many family members, friends, and teachers influenced my interest in education, it was a question from one stranger that kickstarted me into action. I was in my early twenties working at a grocery store and running the express check-out line that afternoon. A man, who appeared to be middle aged, loaded his few items onto the counter, looked me in the eyes, and asked, "Is this what you've always dreamed about doing?" I was shocked, a bit offended, and mumbled something like, "I don't know," while quickly finishing his order. His words lingered as he left and continued replaying in my mind as I drove home that night. I had worked my way up from bagging groceries, stocking shelves, to being a cashier. I enjoyed helping customers, solving problems with colleagues, and looked for ways to continue improving the services that our store provided. However, there were many days that I would watch the clock and count the minutes until my shift was over. I called my dad and explained the situation feeling annoyed by the question and wondering why this stranger would have said anything like that to me. My dad listened to my rant, and then asked, "Well, do you love what you are doing?"

This continued to send me into a spin, "I don't know, Dad!"

He then asked me to think about what I was doing when I was the happiest. That was an easy question to answer. "It's when I'm with kids. It's when I'm learning. It's when I'm helping others."

This empowering encounter sparked my interest to explore college and about four years later, I was walking across the stage to receive my diploma.

Maybe you are in your career because of an influential conversation or an example that piqued your curiosity enough to take a step. How can we start these conversations with students? Empower your students by sharing yourself. Tell your story of how you got where you are in your career and talk about skills and knowledge that you've gained along the way. The closer students get to finishing their K-12 career, the more anxious some will be about their next steps. Students need to know themselves before making informed decisions for their future.

Here's an activity to try with your students. I've added my example in the underlined sentences below. As you read, think of what you would put there to describe your favorite place. Think about one of your favorite places to be. This could be a place that you have visited in the past, one that you continue to visit, or a place that you dream about:

> **One of my favorite places can be** <u>dangerous. One "sneaker" ocean wave taught me the valuable lesson to never turn my back on the sea. You must be on high alert looking for the tide to change. You need to analyze the shoreline to determine if stepping into the water is a good idea or not. When wading in past your ankles, it is important to have the skills to swim.</u>

An experience in my favorite place can feel familiar. You can count on watching the waves going out and coming in, over and over again. You can shut your eyes and hear seagull cries while feeling the wind on your face. There's a salty smell from the ocean spray as you walk barefoot in the sand looking for keepsakes. Even though I've collected cherished family memories from a specific seashore, I can recall these with ease from any ocean that I explore.

The place that you chose to think about most likely reflects your core values in some way and just being there helps you be at your best. You might also find true, good, and beautiful connections, as well. For me, the ocean is a place where I seek adventure (true), where I can feel connected to loved ones (good), and where I'm amazed (beautiful).

Ask your students to think of one of their favorite places to be and help them unpack the reasons why they love being there. How many of their reasons could be categorized as true, good, or beautiful? How might their favorite place be a clue to a career path where they would blossom?

When teachers take their own learning inventory and reflect on their experiences that were either empowering or discouraging, they are positioning themselves well to be a helper to their students. In the book, T*he Helping Relationship Process and Skills* (2003), authors Brammer and MacDonald have sorted helping skills into three categories: *Skills for Understanding*, *Skills For Support and Crisis Intervention*, and *Skills For Positive Action*. The authors explain how each helper must develop an individual style and theory about helping. A helper's theory can be built by activating the following stages:

Stage 1: Reflecting on your own personal experiences. How did you get here?

Stage 2: Read and connect with others.

Stage 3: Remix of your own experiences and those of others.

Empowering every child by meeting them where they are in academic, physical, cognitive, social, and emotional development and supporting them in continued learning is a team effort between home, school, and community. A learner needs to have their brain, heart, and courage taken into consideration when traveling down the K-12 yellow brick road of education. Obstacles will come up, and there will be times to find an alternative path that keeps a learner growing and getting better.

A learner needs to have their brain, heart, and courage taken into consideration when traveling down the K-12 yellow brick road of education.

The ASCD Whole Child Network (2020) shares resources to help schools measure how well they are serving their students based on the following Whole Child Tenets:

- **Healthy** - Each student enters school healthy and learns about and practices a healthy lifestyle.
- **Safe** - Each student learns in an environment that is physically and emotionally safe for students and adults.
- **Engaged** - Each student is actively engaged in learning and is connected to the school and broader community.
- **Supported** - Each student has access to personalized learning and is supported by qualified, caring adults.
- **Challenged** - Each student is challenged academically and prepared for success in college or further study and for employment and participation in a global environment.

We'll look at these Whole Child Tenets of Healthy and Safe in the pages that follow; for now, check out how Plato's quote shared at the beginning of the chapter summarizes the three Whole Child Tenets of Engaged, Supported, and Challenged:

> "Do not train a child to learn by force or harshness..." students are best *supported* through respect and honor; "but direct them to it by what amuses their mind..." students are *engaged* when learning is connected their interests, "that you may better be able to discover with accuracy the peculiar bent of genius in each..." students are *challenged* to learn when their strengths are activated.

Engagement can be found in learning spaces that provide autonomy to students. A learner's autonomy is a powerful motivator and helps students gain confidence to learn and try something independently. My parents encouraged me to learn through discovery and gave me permission to try things on my own. When I became a parent, I realized giving choice to my children and space to discover meant that I had to let go of what I expected the outcome to be. Encouraging students to solve problems and engage their curiosity can be messy.

Early one morning I heard a noise in the kitchen and walked in to find my two-year-old son struggling to hold up a gallon of milk in his little hands. He stood in front of a bowl with two Cheerios in it, and the remainder of the box of cereal had spread across the floor. As I ran to help, he yelled, "MYSELF!" and I stopped, watching him pour a fountain of milk on the floor with some landing in the bowl. Then he happily sat down in the spilled milk, grabbed his spoon, and started eating off the floor. After he finished and "we" cleaned up the floor, I decided to help him find more success with this in the future. Each night before bed, we would pour some cereal into a bowl and set out his spoon. In the refrigerator, there was a small cup of milk for him to use on a shelf that he could easily reach. He was so proud of his ability to make his own breakfast and I was grateful that he had the skills and resources to do this by himself. Learners gain confidence when the following three statements are true:

I have a need
I know where the resources are for this need.
I'll take care of this myself.

About three decades after my toddler's breakfast experiment, I saw the same determined look from my eighteen-month-old grandson during our visit to the ice cream shop. My son, the Cheerios kid, found a highchair for my grandson while my daughter-in-law ordered. Soon my four-year-old granddaughter had a cup of strawberry ice cream with a spoon and was enjoying each bite. My grandson looked back and forth between his "Sissy" and his mom, who had sat next to him with two spoons in a cup of ice cream that they would share. He let out a yell and indicated with body language that he was not interested in sharing a cup of ice cream with his mom. I could see in his eyes the word, "MYSELF." Listening to his determined dissent, my daughter-in-law scooped some ice cream in his own cup, handed him his own spoon, and immediately my grandson relaxed. He smiled as he looked over to his sister, and then took his first bite by himself. Learners can be motivated through situational interest. If these statements are true, then learners might be discovering a new interest:

I can see someone enjoying something that looks interesting to me.
I have decided that I have this need, too.
I'll request the needed resources, so that I can have enjoyment, too.

Empowered learners are eager to try, accept resources and support as needed, and are willing to share their learning with others. Schools are venues where learners should be encouraged to share. Seeing what others are able to do, especially when this brings enjoyment, is a strong motivator for learners. Schools can serve families by providing resources and hosting collaboration events that promote and model engaging learning strategies and activities. A key question to ask when collaborating about how to engage students in their learning is, "What are we doing for the student, that they could be doing independently or with some guidance?" If we know that autonomy is a key to engagement, and that like us, kids are 100% human, we have all that we need to put ourselves in their shoes and navigate one scenario at a time.

Guidance is *support* that empowers because it provides learners with information and resources, without taking away their ownership of the learning. When my teaching shifted from procedural only to involving conceptual understanding in mathematics, I found that my students had different gaps for the needed pre-requisite skills. This was an overwhelming discovery, as I found some students needed to learn order of operations, others had not mastered how to multiply and divide, while still others were ready to work through the required multi-step equations. Math tasks were shared with a team and students would work until they would get stuck. I'd offer some explicit skill instruction for the needed learning, and they would continue. Teachers can involve students by allowing them to help each other. If students have demonstrated understanding, have them communicate their learning with each other. Students can offer valuable feedback when they have resources to self-check for accuracy. Providing time for students to work together is not only empowering, this helps build capacity for needed instructional guidance in the classroom.

Challenge learners through choices and mentor them to list out their pros and cons for decision making. Ask students guiding questions to help them sort what they know, what their challenges are, and what they hope for in their next steps. Let's look at a high school experience through the eyes of our students. Some high school students who are prepared to continue their education, ready to join the workplace, or serve in the military might be looking forward to their senior year. These students have often been supported by adults or peers and have established a plan, even before high school. Other high schoolers are anxious about next steps and are having a hard time connecting themselves to the resources and opportunities available to them. And some high schoolers are simply surviving the day-to-day challenges and life events that are barriers to their current learning situation and their future plans. I can relate most to this group of learners, as I was in my early twenties before I began thinking about my interests and how my next steps would help me thrive, rather than just survive. A question from a stranger, "Is this what you've always wanted to do?" and my *Aha* moment when answering back in my mind, "Wait, I get to choose?"

Empower learners by helping them know their value and how they can use this to contribute in their community. As we challenge students to learn about themselves, we need to have a learning environment that honors diversity. While we are all 100% human, we are also unique. Schools that create systems for students to comply and conform are missing out on the beauty of humanity.

Just Be You

Student-teaching provided me with foundational experiences and resources that I've continued to use throughout my career in education. One of these experiences encouraged me to just be myself. I remember feeling surprised when my cooperating teacher said, "You are talking to the kids with a teacher's voice and not your own." I was? She must have noticed the confusion on my face as I was processing her feedback. She explained that she had once been given the same advice from a principal. The principal suggested that she get a stool to sit on and that this might help her remember that she was just sharing in a conversation with the students. Then my cooperating teacher, who was becoming my mentor, handed me a stool. This prop empowered me to move from performing a role to just being myself with my students.

While you are "being yourself" with learners, let them see you taking care of yourself, as well. I like the idea of "Life-fit" instead of balancing life, as Jimmy Casas shared in his book, *Culturize* (2017), using the following six steps:

1. Be purposeful in scheduling down time.
2. Drop activities that zap your time and energy.
3. Set aside time weekly to do something that you truly enjoy doing and honor it.
4. Consider what you can delegate to someone else.
5. Trust that others will follow through on your expectations.
6. Take care of your body by exercising and making healthy food choices.

One way to bring attention to these "Life-fit" steps is to journal about them. Kami Guarino offers a thoughtful template, with a space to pause before and after work and think about how you can move from surviving to thriving, through her *Resilience Journal: Daily Reflection & Self-Care for Educators (*2019). Taking time to know yourself by discovering your favorite ways to learn, trying strategies that provide you with extra support, and celebrating your learning progress positions you well for empowering others in their learning journeys.

> Activate a process for two-way communication. Learners need to have the ability to opt-out, creating an alternative for themselves if the learning experience is not working well for them.
>
> ~

Remember that you have many partners waiting to help you in your work as a teacher if you choose to invite them. Students can be involved in every part of the learning, from planning of lessons, finding and using resources, research and experimentation, to sharing and feedback.

Activate a process for two-way communication. Learners need to have the ability to opt-out, creating an alternative for themselves if the learning experience is not working well for them. This is true for learners of all ages; how does a district or school allow for teachers to personalize their professional development? Keeping the communication going from teachers to students, and from students to teachers not only helps deepen the learning through rich connections, it's a great way to avoid duplication or unnecessary overlap, giving students an appropriate workload.

When I moved from the classroom to working with adult learners, I noticed that some would apologize for not knowing something. It was a common response when I would share a new technology workflow or help them see a missed step. Embrace the struggle, as this is part of learning. If you are solving problems with your students, your team, or by yourself, know that stumbling and even failing is a lesson from which to grow. These words are easier to accept when you are not in the middle of the disappointment from a mistake or failure. As a young child, I remember feeling so frustrated with myself when I made a mistake that I would literally fall to the floor like a rag doll. My parents would say, "Marita get off of the floor." I would just lay there overwhelmed with all the feelings, and yes, I would be in full "fit mode." Telling people to get over their fit, when they are in the middle of it, isn't helpful. My parents discovered this and gave me a strategy. I was encouraged to feel free to fall apart for up to five minutes in the other room, away from the rest of the family. This strategy helped me acknowledge my feelings and with permission to have the fit, I usually ended up needing less and less time to pull myself together.

Self-regulation is developed and if this isn't mastered before students come to school, then chances are they will need their teachers to help them with strategies for coping with disappointment. When your students struggle, have empathy for where they are, remembering that they are 100% human, just like you are, and might just need time to recover.

As a master learner, you have a fantastic opportunity to show students that not knowing something, or making a mistake, is just evidence that you are learning. Model for your students what learning looks like by admitting when you don't know something. Let your students watch you seek help when help is needed. Students are watching your reactions, your facial expressions, and your coping skills when you struggle. Isn't it a relief to know that we need not be the knower or expert of all things?

Working with others accelerates our learning growth and it also reminds us of our human need to be accepted and belong. While we strive for being a "we," it's important that we don't lose our "I." Some places to watch our students navigate the "we" and the "I" are lunchrooms and playgrounds. During playground duty, I noticed a phenomenon happen year after year. I would see a student walking around the field carrying a clipboard with a piece of paper attached, and a pencil in hand. This kid would be followed by a couple of other kids, usually one on each side. The clipboard carrier was also the question asker, "Would you like to be in my club?" Even as the adult on recess duty, I was asked to be in many such "clubs." My answer was always the same, "What do I need to do to be in your club?" Usually, I'd hear, "Just sign your name, here." Then I would ask, "Who gets to decide who is invited to your club?" and usually the clipboard carrier would say, "I do!"

Another playground duty gem comes to mind, when I think about how even young learners share a need to belong. A student came running up to me, just bursting with excitement. "Guess what?" he yelled. "We just finished doing our project that helped us learn about our ancestors and I'm from Scotland!" Before I could reply, he smiled with pure glee, and said, "Now I know why I love Scottish Cheese!"

We know that students can quickly get themselves into trouble because of their need to belong and sometimes teachers are the first to see the warning signs. As students move from elementary to middle school, and then onto high school the more freedom that they might have to hang out with friends without supervision. It's important that we help students have the courage to get themselves out of a dangerous situation, and that they have trusted adults to help them, as well. Influential educator Rita Pierson said it well during her 2013 TED talk: "Every child deserves a champion, an adult who will never give up on them, who understands the power of connection, and insists that they become the best that they can possibly be." Every student needs to know that their teachers are for them, that they have something valuable to offer, and that school is a better place because they are there.

Activate EMPOWER for Learners

The question at the beginning of this chapter was, "Who is Learning?" The answer is you are, your students are, everyone living is in the process of learning. When you are sharing who you are with others, they might be willing to share who they are with you. Knowing your students, helping them see their value, and guiding them to be lifelong learners who contribute are active ingredients for difference making.

Welcome, This Is A Good Place For You: How are students welcomed into your school for the first time? How about every day after that? What messages are on the walls of the school entrance? Smiles, sights, sounds, and smells? Reflect on your K-12 learning experiences and discover moments when you felt empowered and when you felt discouraged. What do those empowering memories have in common?

100% Human: Who is learning? We are all 100% human at any age and while we are each unique, we share the need to be empowered and acknowledged by another person. Check out Rita Pierson's, "Every kid needs a champion" TED talk (2013) to be inspired and to remember that "you are born to make a difference."

Just Be You: What's the vibe at your school? Do your students know you? Do they know other trusted adults in your school? Give a group of students the opportunity to interview students and staff members asking about what they enjoy at school and what they wish could be different. Use the responses from these student-led interviews to inform changes or to start some action research on how to improve.

Finding the True, Good, and Beautiful

When schools are places where learners are listened to and empowered, then students cannot wait for the doors to be open. Try this activity: Read through the quote below.

> "To all that come to this happy place, welcome. Disneyland is your land. Here age relives fond memories of the past, and here youth may savor the challenge and promise of the future. Disneyland is dedicated to the ideals, the dreams, and the hard facts that have created America...with hope that it will be a source of joy and inspiration to all in the world!"
>
> Walt Disney

Now re-read Disney's quote and imagine your school or district name in place of the word "Disneyland." Would this still be true? Schools and classrooms should share Disney's mission. Can you find true, good, and beautiful represented in the above quote? For an extra challenge, try this activity with your students, families, colleagues, and community members. What would need to change in order to have a welcoming "happy place" that honors the past, present, and looks forward to the future, with hope, joy, and inspiration?

To check on how your team is doing to empower the learners you serve, you can start by asking some questions that connect well with True, Good, and Beautiful:

True	Good	Beautiful
Facts	Connections/ Collaboration	Strengths/Interests
What is the vibe in your learning community? What does learning feel like?	How do learners listen to and connect with each other?	Do your students know that their presence and contributions make a difference, and that they are missed when they are not there?
What does learning sound like and look like?	How do learners empower each other?	Do you know that your presence and contributions matter?

CHAPTER 3

Analyze: What is Learning?

Listen, Empower, ***Analyze,*** *Resources, Needs, Experiences, Relationships*

"A good decision is based on knowledge and not on numbers."
Plato

When schools and districts are making data-driven decisions that are based solely on numbers, they are missing important parts of a learner's story. The *Oath for Learners* helps remind us to **Analyze** and study our students as they learn. If you've been supporting learners for any length of time, you already know that numbers fall short when analyzing students' learning. As mentioned in Plato's quote, we should be making decisions "based on knowledge" and in education we should know who our students are, how they best learn, and what they might be missing in their *Job as a Learner*. This chapter offers insight into how learning measurements and reports could be remixed to incorporate the true, good, and beautiful to gain knowledge about where students are, and how they are making progress. As you read, think about the question, "What is Learning?" The following quote from the documentary *Imagineering Story* (2019), honors the process of growth and discovery:

> "Disneyland will never be completed. It will continue to grow as long as there is imagination left in the world. It is something that will never be finished. Something that I can keep developing and adding to."
>
> Walt Disney

We looked earlier at how schools could learn from Disney's philosophy to create experiences that are welcoming, spark curiosity, and encourage fun. This time let's replace the word "Disneyland" with "Learning" to help us think about honoring and encouraging the process of learning in our schools:

> Learning will never be completed. Learning will continue to grow as long as there is imagination left in this world. Learning is something that will never be finished. Learning is something that I can keep developing and adding to.

During my teacher preparation courses, I learned valuable history, processes, and strategies that I still carry with me today. I've also had to unlearn some techniques or processes in order to provide responsive and relevant learning opportunities for my students.

When coaching teachers and providing technical assistance for integrating technology, I've been fortunate to glean many valuable treasures. One that came from a veteran science teacher put into words the change that happens when a teacher shifts away from allegiance to content toward allegiance to learners.

This experienced high school teacher had wisdom and resources to share with his students that far exceeded textbook learning. His style had been rich with lectures and modeling experiments while providing high level questioning and expecting students to reflect on these offerings. He felt that as long as all eyes were on him and everyone was listening, then learning was guaranteed to happen; however, the evidence from his students would often fall short of his expectations for their growth. He asked me to help him with suggestions about how to engage students in science.

We explored the use of station rotations, partner learning, and small group instruction to meet students where they were in their current understanding and support them in gaining knowledge and skills. We activated technology by putting expectations and resources in a learning management system that would serve as a guide when students were at the Research, Experiment, and Reflection stations. Another station was designed for small group instruction with the teacher as the expert to guide them.

> While it is important to have expertise in the content that you teach, it is also important to have expertise in studying the students, as they, in turn, study the content.

A few weeks later, I received an invitation to come visit this classroom again. Walking in, I was motioned to join the teacher at his desk and together we observed the students. Everyone had a job to do. Some students were studying quietly, others were collaborating around an activity, and others were conducting an experiment. *Learning looked like* students in action. *Learning sounded like* a coffee shop with multiple conversations happening and with some quiet corners that were reserved for deep studying. *Learning felt like* students being empowered and making connections to why their work was valuable. The teacher looked at me, smiled, and said something that I will never forget, "You see, now I study the students, while they study the content." While it is important to have expertise in the content that you teach, it is also important to have expertise in studying the students, as they, in turn, study the content.

In addition to making time to organize learning experiences and observe students at work, it is important to be a learner with them. Learning is contagious. Teachers can create situational interest through their own passions and interests, as enthusiasm also influences the success of the learning happening in a classroom. Remember our students are 100% human and can recognize truth, goodness, and beauty. They know when their teacher's heart is into the work.

The role of a teacher includes helping students discover the "Why?" in their learning. Encourage students to analyze their learning by connecting the learning goal to an action or application, then assist them in reflecting on the value of the knowledge or skill. Some teachers are providing this kind of transparency to learning for their students by displaying it in student-friendly language on a whiteboard in the classroom, or as an overview for lessons that are accessed through a learning management system. Take a look at this fill-in-the-blank sentence that can be used to analyze each learning goal:

> I know (Learning Goal), so that I can (Action or Application), which helps me (Value of Skill/Knowledge).

Add your own words to the blanks with a learning goal that you have for yourself or your students, as in the following example:

> I know how to write a letter, so that I can thank my Grandma for a birthday present, which helps me share a note with someone I love.

Do you see the true, good, and beautiful in the example? As you look further into this **Analyze** chapter, revisit the table at the end of the chapter to see how bringing all three of these elements together can provide learners with a comprehensive education experience.

A Remix for Measuring and Reporting Learning

Time is a precious commodity and, because of this, school systems have developed benchmarks to encourage achievement based on the age of the student and the month of the calendar. While there is something to be said for getting things on the calendar as a way to ensure progress, the one-size-fits-all delivery and assessment of learning is not providing optimal conditions for all learners. Time has been one universal way that our education system has measured learning, along with the focus for grading student work. Do calendars and bell schedules get more attention than analyzing the growth and development of each student who is part of your team?

Education can be a nimble and responsive service to support students in their natural learning growth and development, while providing experiences and activities that inspire students to learn and contribute, using what they've learned. This kind of service requires educators to see learning as a continuum, analyzing what is essential for students to know and be able to do. They must also have a passion for their customers—the students they serve. This kind of education service incorporates choice, feedback, respect, trust, and love for the people being served.

Great teachers are masters of learning; they love learning and get excited when they see others learn. How our education system certifies and evaluates teachers should align with how we hope to serve our students. If the way that we analyze data ranks and sorts our learners and then connects their achievements to rewards or penalties, success is limited to only some of those we serve—or hire to serve—our students. Learning doesn't take a break for summer or stop after walking across the stage to receive a diploma. Learning is a lifelong human opportunity and we do this best when we are valued and realize that we have something valuable to offer others. Benjamin Bloom's (1968) research shared in the 20th Century shined light on the fact that all students can learn and, in fact, most students can learn to high levels of mastery, given appropriate support and adequate time. When time and support are analyzed and adjusted to serve students where they are, then learning can be accessible to all.

As educators change conversations away from a year's worth of knowledge in a year's time, to continual learning for a lifetime, how will we measure success in learning for all students? One measure of success could be to look at the *Job of a Learner*. Twenty years into the 21st Century has given us a clear vision into the fact that as humans, we need to be able to learn, adapt, and learn some more in order to succeed in this world. There is not a comprehensive curriculum or sufficient list of standards that, even if learned to mastery, will guarantee success for the future. We know that learning is a timeless commodity that will serve our students well, so let's take a look at the *Job of the Learner* and see how this connects to *An Oath for Learners.*

Job of a Learner

Listen: I want to learn because of my own curiosity or because I think it is valuable to me.
Empower: I believe in my own abilities to learn.
Analyze: I reflect on what I know, what I hope to learn, or what I've learned.
Resources: I ask for help or know where to find help.
Needs: I understand how I best learn and ask for help when needed.
Experiences: I learn by asking questions, collaborating, investigating, experimenting, creating...
Relationships: I work with others to share my learning or learn from them.

If we measure how the learner is doing their job, then we are measuring the learning process, rather than a product. When we add a teacher, who is activating learning through growth and development, as mentioned in the *Oath for Learners*, and has support from their school or district to offer education as a service, then we have a new formula for measuring learning success.

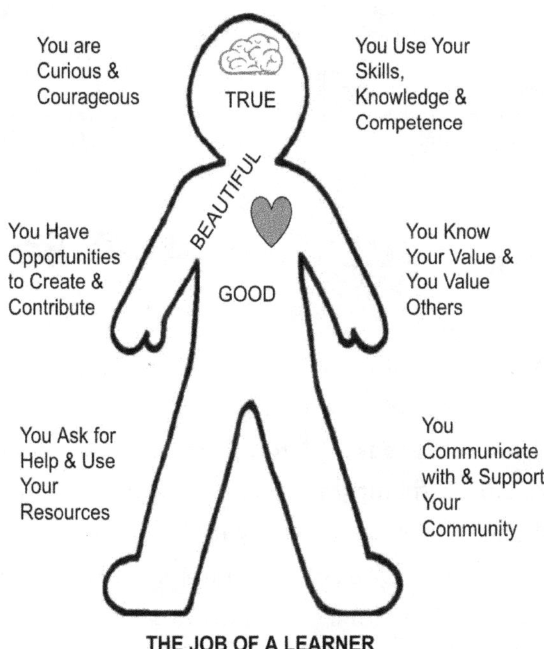

THE JOB OF A LEARNER

Listen, **E**mpower, **A**nalyze, **R**esources, **N**eeds, **E**xperiences, **R**elationships

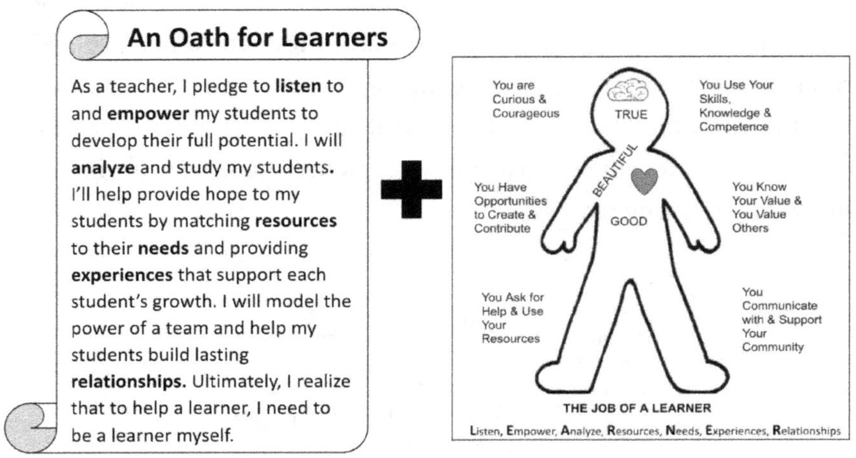

Education As A Service

Our current educational system of ranking and sorting may determine success for some learners, but not for all. Humans can't be standardized and this makes determining success for all within our education system a difficult thing to measure. While data trends can be useful to tell part of the success story for a system, they can be equally harmful to an individual learner. The numbers that we use to determine learning success for individuals come from a flawed data system based on averages. Providing required benchmarks such as expectations for kindergarten readiness, third grade reading scores, and ninth grade Algebra classes do not, on their own, ensure that students learn.

Growth and development needs to be incorporated into each learner's educational journey, helping them tell the story of their progress. When our school system focuses only on what can be quantified, then we miss out on providing meaningful feedback to our students. Meaningful feedback for supporting the whole child consists of all three of Plato's ways of knowing. I found a treasure from the past, my husband's kindergarten report card and, with his permission, I'm sharing some of this in the table below. In the left column, you'll find the Kindergarten Report Card from the 20th Century, and in the right column, you'll see a 21st Century Kindergarten Report Card from the same school district. In both columns, I've noted where the True, Good, and Beautiful might connect to the expectation that is being reported on.

Kindergarten Report Card (Two Different Centuries, Same District)

20th Century	21st Century
Frequency: Report card provided twice a year (2nd quarter, and 4th quarter)	Frequency: Report card shared three times a year (2nd, 3rd, 4th quarters),
Data Represented as a checklist with feedback given as "Yes, Sometimes, Not Yet" for specific skills in the following areas:	Data collected through grading symbols: O = Outstanding S = Satisfactory N = Needs improvement U = Unsatisfactory = standard met, ✓ = Standard nearly met, - = Standard not met
The following is a compare/contrast of content and subject areas reported, along with headings and subheadings. I've analyzed both sides by labeling *True, Good, Beautiful* after each area that was being reported.	

Growth in Knowledge, Skills, and Understanding	
Language Arts • Speaks clearly and accurately *(True)* • Uses adequate vocabulary *(True)* • Is confident in front of a group (*Good)* • Uses complete sentences *(True)*	Listening and Speaking • Speaks in complete sentences *(True)*
Handwriting • Recognizes own name *(True)* • Writes own name *(True)* • Has adequate control of crayons and pencils *(True)*	Writing • Uses drawing, dictating, and writing to express ideas *(Beautiful)* • Uses phonetic spelling in daily writing *(True)*
Science • Is curious about and interested in his surroundings *(Beautiful)* • Remembers and puts to use new learnings and vocabulary *(True)*	Science - Not reported
Art • Enjoys a variety of materials *(Beautiful)* • Expresses his own ideas through creative art *(Beautiful)* • Handles scissors correctly *(True)* • Knows and names the colors *(True)*	Art - Not reported

Reading Readiness • Enjoys books, stories, and poems *(Beautiful)* • Can tell a story in proper sequence *(True)* • Participates in create dramatics *(Beautiful)* • Can see likenesses and differences in objects, pictures, letters *(True)*	Reading • Identifies uppercase and lowercase in any order *(True)* • Identifies letter sounds *(True)* • Reads sight words *(True)* • Identifies rhyming words *(True)* • Sounds out/Reads words *(True)* • Text Reading Level *(True)*
Number Readiness • Recognizes numerals *(True)* • Writes numerals *(True)* • Counts with understanding *(True)* • Uses number skills in daily activities *(True)* • Can see likenesses and differences in shapes, sizes, and amounts *(True)* • Knows own address and telephone number *(True)*	Mathematics Orally counts to 100 *(True)* Counts objects to 20 *(True)* Recognizes number 0-20 out of order *(True)* Writes numbers to 20 *(True)* Solves simple addition problems *(True)* Solves simple subtraction problems *(True)* Identifies geometric shapes *(True)*
Citizenship • Takes part in group activities *(Good)* • Contributes ideas to group discussions *(Good)* • Has a growing understanding of his surroundings *(Good)*	Citizenship - Not reported
Music • Enjoys listening to music *(Beautiful)* • Enjoys and participates in rhythms *(Beautiful)* • Enjoys and participates in singing *(Beautiful)* • Remembers words to songs *(Beautiful)*	Music - Not reported

Personal and Social Growth	
Social Attitudes • Shares and takes turns *(Good)* • Uses self-control *(Good)* • Respects authority *(Good)* • Accepts responsibility *(Good)* • Claims only his share of attention *(Good)* • Respects the rights and property of others *(Good)* • Accepts constructive criticism *(Good)*	Social and Behavioral Development Follows classroom/playground rules *(Good)* Respects authority and property of others *(Good)*
Work Habits • Works independently *(True)* • Completes work begun *(True)* • Accepts responsibility for clean-up *(Good)* • Can successfully follow more than one direction *(True)*	Work Habits Stays on task and uses time efficiently *(True)* Follows directions *(True)* Returns completed homework *(True)*
Health and Safety Practices • Rests quietly *(True)* • Takes care of wraps *(Good)* • Takes care of personal needs *(True)* • Understands and practices safety rules *(Good)* • Keeps reasonably neat and clean *(True)*	Health and Safety Practices - not reported
Physical Education • Seems physically fit *(True)* • Shows good sportsmanship *(Good)* • Has adequate coordination *(True)* • Participates in group games *(Good)* • Shows adequate muscle development *(True)*	Physical Development Demonstrates large muscle coordination - run, jump, hop, skip *(True)* Demonstrates small muscle coordination - cut, color, write - *(True)*

Parent Reply: Andy loves school! Will work on the "not yets." Message from Superintendent: "We sincerely hope that your child is having an enjoyable and worthwhile year in kindergarten. Kindergarten is intended to provide your child with opportunities for learning that will be beneficial to him this year and in the future."	Parent Reply: Not a place for parents to comment back on the report card. Message from Superintendent: Not included
If you agree with how I've labeled each reporting topic with True, Good, and Beautiful, here are the findings from each column.	
True - 26 Good - 16 Beautiful - 9 Total Reporting Topics = 51 Includes Citizenship, Health and Safety Practices, Music, Art Focus on Growth, Enjoyment	True - 20 Good - 2 Beautiful - 1 Total Reporting Topics = 23

The chart shows how reporting topics have been cut by more than half for the 21st Century Report Card and topics that could be labeled as Good or Beautiful are the areas that were removed. Removing reporting and feedback from subject areas such as *Citizenship, Health, and Safety Practices, Music, Art,* even if these are still being taught, gives a message that they are less important than those that are included on the report card. The above example is one school district's comparison over time and while other districts and schools may be different, there's a strong possibility that this is representative of what has happened in response to standardizing education.

Let's use the garage cleaning analogy to further analyze the difference between the 20th Century and 21st Century report cards. Take a look at the following questions and add your own observations:

What was kept as an essential topic to report on?

- *Overall feedback for a student's achievement level, at the time of the reporting.*
-

What was kept and repurposed?

- *A 20th Century checklist with feedback given as: "Yes, Sometimes, Not Yet" changed to 21st Century Grading Symbols that represent, Outstanding, Satisfactory, Needs Improvement, Unsatisfactory or + standard met, ✓ = Standard nearly met, - = Standard not met*
-

What was put off to the side that students may still experience, but is not reported?

- *Citizenship, Health, and Safety Practices, Music, Art were not on the 21st Century report card.*
-

What is missing?

- *A place for parents to reply*
- *Focus on Growth and Enjoyment*
-

The comparison of these report cards provides insight into two major shifts in education that I've experienced as a learner, parent, teacher, and administrator between the 20th and 21st Century. First, a standardized way of reporting, rather than reporting growth for an individual. Second, a standardized way of instructing, with grade level benchmarks provided through standardized state tests. Standardization was designed to measure grade level achievement within our K-12 educational system. Policymakers have used data to see what system resources might be needed, and researchers used the standardized data to study the success of our education system. The promise of standardization to provide an equitable learning experience for all learners has not held true. Ironically, it is standardization that has hindered providing feedback on the "Good and the Beautiful" in education, as these are difficult to quantify and create averages for.

There is, however, a collective effort to bring these back into the service of education. In 2019, an Aspen Institute report titled, "From a Nation at Risk to a Nation of Hope," (2019, p. 33) provided six recommendations for Social, Emotional, and Academic Development, explaining "The promotion of social, emotional, and academic learning is not a shifting educational fad; it is the substance of education itself." The six recommendations are as follows:

1. Set a clear vision that broadens the definition of student success to prioritize the whole child.
2. Transform learning settings so they are safe and supportive for all young people.
3. Change instruction to teach students social, emotional, and cognitive skills; embed these skills in academics and schoolwide practices.
4. Build adult expertise in child development.
5. Align resources and leverage partners in the community to address the whole child.
6. Forge closer connections between research and practice by shifting the paradigm for how research gets done.

Now let's look one more time at the above report card examples and choose one for yourself, your child, or your grandchild. What feedback would you like to receive? What feedback encourages and motivates you more? What feedback compares yourself to your previous learning journey? What feedback compares you to another learner? How is the report card that you chose valuable to you?

Use the following sentence to capture your thinking or reflection about providing an environment where learning could be a constant, with time as the variable.

> I used to know____________, then I discovered or experienced____________. Now I understand______________.

Here's my reflection about grading and providing feedback:

> I **used to know** that grade point averages measured a student's success, **then I discovered and experienced** how grading practices, including averaging, bonus points, and penalizing late assignments could skew grade point averages and miss the mark when reporting a student's learning success. **Now I understand** that grading should be feedback of the learning for each student and based on evidence that learning targets were reached at a level of proficiency or mastery.

Learning and Leading

When education is a service, leaders spend time analyzing system resources, relationships, and responses to ensure that these are valuable to learners. Great education leaders observe learning from a variety of vantage points to assess their team's success and needs. Reflecting back to Plato's quote, "A good decision is based on knowledge and not on numbers," demonstrates that leaders need to spend time in the learning arena with those that they serve.

Learning from horses during an Equine Field Trip with fellow administrators in my Education Specialist program was an unexpected surprise. Our professor, Dr. Heather Williams, had set up a half-day simulation to help us learn about ourselves, as system leaders and learners.

The sixteen of us entered the arena on a chilly fall morning to greet our "students," about a half dozen horses. Two from our team were horse owners, and immediately walked up to the horses with confidence and care. The rest of us awkwardly stood in the middle of the arena together, as we were told that we had the common goal to get all of our "students" through the two posts, that were positioned wide enough for a few horses to walk through at the same time.

Dr. Williams and the Equine Therapy facility staff came around to each of us and shared instructions for our individual jobs. I was told to move the horses clockwise around the arena at least once, and then to guide them through the posts to their "graduation." Everyone began to approach the horses and it was obvious that we had been given different directions, which created mixed messages for our "students." The horses had nothing on them, no halters, saddles, bits, or leads. Our group tried a variety of strategies to make the horses go in the direction that we had been instructed but after ten minutes, we had made no progress. We had just confused the horses, who tried to huddle up with each other, and the rest of us were either shouting, clapping hands wildly, trying to pull the horses in a direction, or giving up altogether.

Things got heated when two from our cohort moved the posts, in order to have all the horses go through them. While some thought that was an acceptable adjustment, others became furious at the gesture, explaining that this was lowering the bar. Meanwhile, one person just kept walking one horse around the arena, cradling its head in her arm, as she led it through the posts, again and again. It was all a little chaotic before our professor eventually asked us to exit the arena and we worked together to analyze the situation from a different angle. In our debrief, some shared about feeling bad for the horses, others talked about ways that we could have reached our goal together, and a few explained that we would not have found success until we all got on the same page.

After having lunch, a second challenge was waiting for us in the arena. This time we were put into teams, given specific roles to play, and a specific horse to work with. We had an obstacle course to get our horse through, where each person was stationed at each obstacle. I was given the role of a "superintendent" who would provide oversight and guidance to my team and our horse, as we attempted the course. I was only allowed to share verbal instructions with my team members, because my feet were to stay within the boundary of a hula hoop that was placed on the ground. There were 4 or 5 of us in this role and we each had 3-4 team members stationed throughout the course. The "superintendent" to my right immediately picked up his hula hoop from the ground and started walking around to quietly visit with each of his team members. The other "superintendents" and I did not appreciate his interpretation of the rules; however, another "supt" also started scooting his hula hoop to help him move around.

As I analyzed the response that my team's horse was giving, it became clear that she couldn't understand what we were asking of her. We needed something to lead the horse. I pulled off my scarf and tied it around our horse's neck and then helped our "student" complete the obstacle closest to me. As we handed the horse and scarf off to the next team member, our "student" followed and completed each activity in the obstacle with ease. Soon other teams were shedding their coats and outer shirts to create similar leads, and, aha! We all found success! We just needed to communicate with the horses in a way that they would understand. We also needed to be in agreement and to have confidence in ourselves and our team. This time the horses relaxed and didn't retreat to the corner of the arena, away from us. This time we analyzed our situation while standing together inside the arena. Some of the horses stood close to us, as if we were all in a team huddle together. We achieved the power of agreement that can only come from shared understanding, respect, and synchronized action.

> Effective leadership can be recognized by the trusting relationships that the team shares and the progress that they make together toward the strategic goals.
>
> 

This equine-assisted learning experience provided insight into how we worked as individuals and as a team when it came to communication and trust. Dr. Williams (2020) explains in her research, "People can sometimes say one thing, but their body language and facial expressions say something completely different. Horses detect this inconsistency because it breaks their trust, which results in them taking actions to move toward safety." Effective leadership can be recognized by the trusting relationships that the team shares and the progress that they make together toward the strategic goals.

Analyzing learning should include evidence of academic skills and knowledge gained, along with social and emotional growth. In the arena, there was much more going on than just getting the horses through the goalposts. In our schools and classrooms, there is true, good, and beautiful to be found in learning that can't be accurately formulated on a spreadsheet. Throughout the time of my Ed.S. study, the following statement was repeated in various learning scenarios and simulations: "We are unable to measure what is most important for learning." If we continue to measure success with artificial averages and benchmarks, this statement will be true. If strategic goals that support decision making include analyzing how resources, relationships, and responses support learning, we could find the true, good, and beautiful in our education service. Let's unpack lessons from the above equine field trip to see if we can find all three ways of knowing:

Analyzing Resources - (True)

Use experience as a resource: Some administrators had experience with horses prior to our equine field trip. This not only gave them credibility with their peers, it provided them with the confidence and care needed to accomplish the goals. When making strategic decisions, leaders need to find the experts among them to help determine the skills and support that are needed for learning to happen. Leaders can find these experts serving in their classrooms, lunchrooms, driving their busses, dropping off students at school, and working in their communities. Great leaders spent their time discovering learning needs and filling these needs with the expertise from their team and their greater community.

Use observation as a resource: When developing skills, learners benefit from watching others. Lead learners use observations to determine how learners best learn and what is hindering them from learning. Great leaders provide observation decks through social media venues, newsletters, and school tours to share the treasured learning that is happening. Giving community members a window into the greatness happening in schools is a win-win; keep reading as we look at how learning is a return on investment.

Analyzing Relationships - (Good)

Be Aware of Us vs. Them: In the above example, the horses (our "students") huddled together when they didn't understand their part to play with us. As leaders in the arena, we found more success through community, rather than through competition. Once we had success together, the horses joined us in the middle of the arena to be near us. When learners know that they are included in the culture of the school, that the school is a better place because they are there, that they have something to offer, then they will want to share. Learners are willing to try new things and will develop confidence in themselves when they see that those helping them learn truly believe in them.

Be Aware of Mixed Messages: Avoid mixed messages by knowing students' needs and interests in order to help them connect to why learning goals are needed and valuable. The expectations for how to use content, processes, and tools need to make sense to the learner. In addition to clarity, leaders should work with their teams to analyze how learning expectations are attainable and appropriate for each learner that they serve.

Analyzing Responses (Beautiful)

Create Two-Way Communication for Learning: Remembering that empowerment inspires learning, lead learners can provide explicit skill instruction through modeling that involves two-way communication. Not just watch me, but join me. Great leaders are trust builders, providing a safe landscape for others to offer opinions, questions, and to share their learning.

Create Opportunities for Equity in Learning: Involve learners, families, and the education support team when creating ways to adapt or modify the learning goal without lowering the bar. All can learn; when there is a will, there is a way.

Learning and leading is evident in a team when coaching and mentoring exists and are used as processes to inspire collaboration, communication, creativity, and critical thinking. Simon Sinek, author of *Start with Why*, explains that, "Leading is not the same as being the leader. Being the leader means you hold the highest rank, either by earning it, good fortune, or navigating internal politics. Leading, however, means that others willingly follow you - not because they have to, not because they are paid to, but because they want to." (Sinek, 2009, p. 65). Strong education teams analyze strengths and weaknesses of team members along with activating family, community, and industry partnerships to ensure relevant learning connections for their students. Strong education teams have experienced both victories and losses together, which ultimately means that the team gets in the arena and learns together. When leaders make decisions based only on numbers, then they are truly missing the greatness of learning.

As a leader, what does it feel like to be analyzed as you are learning? Think of the last time that you fell down. If you were in a public place, chances are the first concern that came to mind was that someone saw you fall. Then you checked for broken bones and blood. Leaders need to be supported and given space and grace to learn. Media and the overall organizational structure of leadership expectations can make a leader feel as if they have no safety net to fall into when they are learning. Lack of learning is what keeps some leaders maintaining the status quo, rather than updating and changing system resources, relationships, and responses to support learners.

When you are supporting learners, you are a leader, whether you hold a leadership title or not. To best help learners, you need to be continually learning. Surround yourself with people who encourage your learning. If you are looking for a professional learning experience to develop your Personal Learning Community that engages you as a learner while growing you as a leader, check out an EdCamp. The purpose of an EdCamp is to provide a learning venue where educators analyze and discuss topics that they are interested in. I've had the opportunity to participate and learn from awesome educators at EdCamp Idaho events for the past seven years. EdCamps encourage attendees to analyze how the sessions are supporting their learning. It's a common practice to use the rule of two feet, and politely leave the room if the session isn't meeting your learning needs or goals. While this might not work as well in a staff meeting or district professional development event, it is an agreed upon practice in EdCamp settings.

Our *Oath for Learners* ends with "I realize that to help a learner, I need to be a learner myself." Being your authentic self will help others give you grace when you stumble. Your learning and leading will thrive when you know yourself and see life as a venue for continued growth. Reflect on how you are doing as a learner and this will help you know how you are doing as a leader. Our learning growth is limited when we stay within our comfort zones. Jump in the arena, learn alongside the people you support, and you will find greatness.

Learning is the Return on Investment

Bridging what students are learning in school with what they will need in order to be employable and successful in the world is a tall order, but a necessary one. Learning is the return on investment and education is a relevant and valuable service when it considers community, learner, and educator requests.

Responding to community requests requires miles in the car, scheduled meetings, and casual conversations with those outside of the education field to learn about what skills and knowledge are needed. In my current role, I've been given the opportunity to connect with employers to ask what they are looking for when hiring employees. Three common responses connect with our TGB theme. Employers are looking for employees to show up and be present (True), get along with others (Good), adapt and learn (Beautiful).

Responding to a learner's request requires a school welcoming plan, along with structures in place to capture ongoing input for needs, ideas, and questions that students have. If I could summarize what I've heard from students, my own children, and reflect on myself as a learner, these would be the top three questions. Why does this matter to me? (True); How will I use this to help myself, my family, friends, community? (Good); How will I share my strengths and interests through this? (Beautiful). Ultimately, learners and their parents hope that their teachers and education support will see them, know them, and help them with learning that makes a difference.

Responding to a teacher's request requires analyzing how existing systems are working to best support learning and teaching. Many years teaching in the classroom, along with providing ongoing support for educators throughout the system has provided me with insight to educational bridges that are in need of repair. As a teacher, I found that the way that we measured learning wasn't helpful to all learners (True); A question that I carried with me throughout each day and even through some nights was, "How can I support each learner, and still meet grade level expectations?" (Good); I was most successful teaching when I had freedom to meet learners where they were, supported them from there, and celebrated their individual learning growth (Beautiful).

Schools can be like gardens where individual learning is cultivated and analyzed to ensure growth for every learner. Schools should not be on a competitive racetrack, where learners line up at the same starting line and where the winners are those who finish first. Each student begins differently because they come with their own background knowledge and experiences. Once a teacher discovers where each student's starting line is, then it's time to provide opportunity, encouragement, connections, and resources to help them in their unique "dash" or process of learning. Consider how the following poem connects to how we might analyze learning in our schools:

The Dash

by Linda Ellis (2006)

I read of a man who stood to speak at the funeral of a friend. He referred to the dates on the tombstone from the beginning... to the end.

He noted that first came the date of birth and spoke of the following date with tears, but he said what mattered most of all was the dash between those years.

For that dash represents all the time they spent alive on earth and now only those who loved them know what that little line is worth.

For it matters not, how much we own, the cars... the house... the cash. What matters is how we live and love and how we spend our dash.

So, think about this long and hard; are there things you'd like to change? For you never know how much time is left that still can be rearranged.

To be less quick to anger and show appreciation more and love the people in our lives like we've never loved before.

If we treat each other with respect and more often wear a smile... remembering that this special dash might only last a little while.

So, when your eulogy is being read, with your life's actions to rehash, would you be proud of the things they say about how you lived your dash?

How does our educational system measure the "dash" in a student's learning? What happens between the pretest and the posttest? The "dash" represents the process of learning as well as growth and development. It is a moving target making it difficult to quantify; it cannot be averaged or compared with other learners' dashes. When we are looking for the true, good, and beautiful in each person, this gets us closer to seeing their dash, or their learning process.

Design and develop your school to be a place that helps learners discover their talents and supports them in solving problems they are interested in solving. Analyze with your team what learning looks like, sounds like, and feels like in your school. Look at how learning is honored, celebrated, and encouraged. Is learning considered a process involving change, with learners doing the work and the growing? Here are some additional topics to explore when analyzing learning as a return on your school's investment:

Customer Satisfaction: Who are the customers in a school? In addition to having formal ways to collect how students and their families are experiencing learning with the school, discovering community perceptions can provide an additional measure for success.

Curate and Share the Learning: Do teachers and leaders share their purpose and interests with students? Where do your students learn the most? Capturing these places and moments with photos and posting on the school's social media gives students, staff, parents, and your community a view into the important work that is happening each day.

Community Listening Posts: The purpose of these events is to provide an opportunity for parents, community members, students, staff and other interested parties to listen to learning stories. This is a great place to celebrate learning. Have the listening go both ways by inviting community members to share their ideas for education. This valuable exchange will help to align educational goals with the needs in the workplace and throughout the community.

Calculating Learning: Meet with your students to review their learning data. Together, look for trends and patterns to support decisions for essential learning targets. Help students prepare reports and reflections to share with their families. Having a process for actionable feedback that makes the next step in reaching the learning target clear is a rewarding experience for both the learner and the teacher. When a learner sets a goal over and above the essential target and reaches it, this is especially rewarding. Consider giving students space to dream beyond the "have to."

> Having a process for actionable feedback that makes the next step in reaching the learning target clear is a rewarding experience for both the learner and the teacher.
>
> ~

Focusing on customer satisfaction, curating learning, community connections, and calculating individual learning growth, results in education becoming a service to inspire and support learning. While the passing of time does not guarantee learning, the good news is that the "needle" is always moving when learning is happening. Our role as participants in the education system is to inspire our learners to learn. When the *Oath for Learners* is activated by a teacher, and the *Job of a Learner* is accomplished by a student, learning happens. The following visual shows how as an educational system, educators, and learners can work together to provide a service of education that will result in preparing students to be lifelong learners and contributors in the world. When learners know the part they play, they can reflect on their learning progress. Take the mystery out of what goes on behind the scenes in education, by having the *Job of a Learner* as a visual in front of students, alongside what their school and their teachers are striving to provide for them. When students realize that school is working for them, rather than thinking that they are working for school, learning flows. This kind of transparency is not only empowering for students, it is a great place to start when measuring learning success.

Education as a Service to Inspire and Support Learning

An Oath to Our Learners *(What Learners Can Expect From Us)*
We will create an education service that **L**istens, **E**mpowers, **A**nalyzes, provides **R**esources, understands your **N**eeds, designs **E**xperiences, and offers caring **R**elationships.

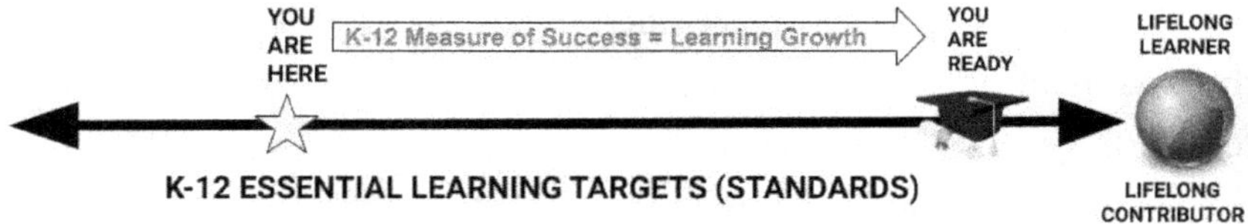

Your Job as a Learner *(What We Expect From Learners)*
Listen: I want to learn because of my own curiosity or because I think it is valuable to me.
Empower: I believe in my own abilities to learn.
Analyze: I reflect on what I know, what I hope to learn, or what I've learned.
Resources: I ask for help or know where to find help.
Needs: I understand how I best learn and ask for help when needed.
Experiences: I learn by asking questions, collaborating, investigating, experimenting, creating
Relationships: I work with others to share my learning or learn from them.

Activate ANALYZE for Learners

Throughout this chapter, we have been analyzing the question, "What is Learning?" To help answer this we looked at how to measure learning, the role of leadership in learning, and how to support the learner. The visual shared at the end of the chapter offers a guide for continued study and analysis about what learners can expect from the service of education, what the job of a learner includes, along with looking at learning growth as a measure of success.

A Remix for Measuring and Reporting Learning: Find ways to study your students while they study the content. How does your feedback process provide flexibility for students to respond, revise, and get additional instructional support? Who is working harder, you or your students? Map this out with your students and find a way to share the load. Activate your team's strengths and support each other's weaknesses. Encourage students to engage their curiosity and share their interests by giving them opportunities to create, self-discover, and experiment.

Review the six recommendations from "From a Nation at Risk, to a Nation at Hope" (2019, pg.33):

The six recommendations are as follows:

1. Set a clear vision that broadens the definition of student success to prioritize the whole child.
2. Transform learning settings so they are safe and supportive for all young people.
3. Change instruction to teach students social, emotional, and cognitive skills; embed these skills in academics and schoolwide practices.
4. Build adult expertise in child development.

5. Align resources and leverage partners in the community to address the whole child.
6. Forge closer connections between research and practice by shifting the paradigm for how research gets done.

What is available to your students? What is missing? Is there something that you'd like to learn more about?

Leading and Learning:
When you hold a mirror up to see yourself as a learner, ask...

- What are my strengths and limitations?
- How do I share my interests and strengths with my students, my work team, my community?
- What interrupts my learning?

What does professional learning look like in your district or school? The changes that you hope to see in the classroom to support students' ownership in their learning, should be visible in professional development offerings.

Explore the EdCamp model for your professional learning, where the experts are the people in the room, you included! Discover ways to provide purpose, encouragement, celebration, and community voice.

Check out this website to get started:
https://sites.google.com/view/edcampidaho/home

Learning As the Return on Investment: Milestones matter! Do your students know the learning targets? Take time to celebrate and reflect on milestones reached. Look at how students might make their learning goals over and above the "essential learning targets." Do the learning activities offered in class align to the learning goals? Does the alignment/connections make sense to students?

Consider involving your students in the creation of learning activities or lessons.

This QR Code will take you to the article, *Tips and Tools for Involving Students in Lesson Planning and Content Delivery*:

Put dates on the calendar for Community Listening Posts. These are great events to celebrate learning and show the return on the investment of school and education.

Finding the True, Good, and Beautiful

Do learners know that they have a job to do? Watch learners move from passive to active learning as they get the big picture of what is going on in school that is designed for them. As you introduce the *Job of the Learner* with learners, show them what they can expect from you through the *Oath for Learners*.

Your Job as a Learner *(What We Expect From Learners)***:**
Listen: I want to learn because of my own curiosity or because I think it is valuable to me.
Empower: I believe in my own abilities to learn.
Analyze: I reflect on what I know, what I hope to learn, or what I've learned.
Resources: I ask for help or know where to find help.
Needs: I understand how I best learn and ask for help when needed.
Experiences: I learn by asking questions, collaborating, investigating, experimenting, and creating.
Relationships: I work with others to share my learning or learn from them.

Frequent and expected learning check-ups can provide time for goal setting, reflection, and guidance for next steps. Involve students in their learning check-ups and realize that success for these will come through the trusting relationships that you share with each other. When we analyze learning for a student, it is as personal as the experience that you have when getting feedback during a medical checkup. There is a "diagnosis" that helps the student see where they currently are, based on "symptoms," or the evidence of the student's learning. From this information there are many "treatment" options for the student to help them move forward or continue practicing until learning happens. During a learning checkup, students are given preventive options on how to avoid distractions to their learning. Ultimately, like feedback from a medical check-up, the way that we analyze and support our students should help them improve, along with providing a place to celebrate milestones. Learning check-ups are really coaching or mentoring sessions that should incorporate all three ways of knowing (true, good, and beautiful) in order to provide complete support for our learners. These learning check-ups should include time for students to reflect and capture the purpose of their learning goal(s) with a TGB fill-in-the-blank sentence like the following:

I know ____________so that I can__________________, which helps me__________________.

True	**Good**	**Beautiful**
Resources	Relationships	Responses
Knowledge	**Skills**	**Dispositions/ Character**
I Know...	So That I Can...	Which Helps Me...

CHAPTER 4

Resources: How Will Learning Continue?

Listen, Empower, Analyze, ***Resources,*** *Needs, Experiences, Relationships*

"Wonder is the beginning of the desire to know the beautiful and the good."

Plato

Learners of all ages have wonder and play as natural resources. Schools can offer adaptable learning spaces as valuable resources. Teachers can be an essential resource by providing relevant instruction and specific feedback to help every student reach their learning goals. If the system of education was a theater, wonder and play would be on the main stage with learners, and the K-12 learning continuum (standards/goals) would be the backdrop. Then, teachers could work behind the scenes to change the "backdrop" as needed to ensure that the show, "learning" continued to go on for each student. There would be times when teachers would join learners on the stage to provide instruction and feedback as students learned through their natural resources of wonder and play.

Using this analogy, we see how teachers can set in motion *An Oath for Learners* by spending some time as audience members where they **Listen** to their students, **Empower** them with an "Encore, Encore!" and then **Analyze** the performance to see if a second take (more instruction) is needed, or if the backdrop can change because students have demonstrated understanding and application of content. In this **Resources** chapter, rather than creating a shopping list, we will think about ways to help our students nurture their sense of wonder by providing them with learning spaces to explore and play and guiding them in bundling their skill sets to move their wonders into actions that make a difference in their lives.

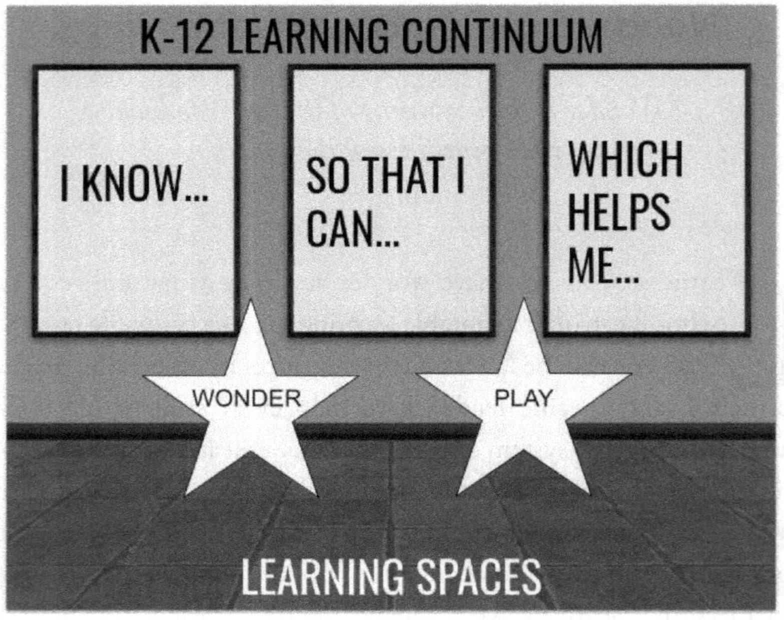

Wonder and Play

You are shipwrecked on a desert island and can only have three items; what would they be? This is a familiar scenario that most of us have answered with items that would care for our basic needs, such as water, food, and protection. In the previous chapter, we analyzed how all three ways of knowing (the true, good, and beautiful) are essential in education. What resources can best provide access to all three? At the beginning of this chapter, Plato's quote explains that "Wonder" is a pathway for good and beautiful. In my experience, the action that is most joyful and that often follows wonder, is play. If we could only have a few resources to nurture in a classroom, wonder and play would be at the top of my list.

Trying to describe in words the important human emotion that we call wonder is difficult. Wonder can be found in an experience that catches your breath, speeds up your heart rate, or challenges your thinking. When we are too quick to discover the facts about something by heading to Google, we might bypass our thinking, our prediction, or even our personal connections. While it's great to help learners know where to find information, it is beneficial to encourage them to wonder first. Wonder is a natural resource that learners carry with them and that has been influenced by their background knowledge and experiences. Teachers can be fantastic wonder coaches by asking questions, and helping learners unpack their thinking prior to getting into new information.

My mom has been my primary wonder coach. She is also a master learner who acts on her curiosity. While healing from cancer, she spent time on her couch reading and dreaming of Italy, a country that she had always wanted to visit. Above her mantle hung a gorgeous painting of Portofino. She talked about this place and wondered what it would be like to stand in that exact spot. When she was strong enough to travel, we planned a trip to Portofino and we stood in that exact same spot; in fact, we jumped in that exact same spot and celebrated life and dreams. My husband and I enjoyed our whirlwind Italian adventure with my mom and stepdad. They played hard and at one point even sprinted up the stairs after a long day of walking around Rome. The owner of the Bed and Breakfast where we were staying noticed their youthfulness and pulled me aside to ask their age. When I told him, his eyes widened, and he exclaimed, "No way!" Then, he followed up by saying something profound, "Your parents are staying young, because they are curious." He went on to explain how he wished his mom hadn't lost her curiosity, because doing this stops a person from learning and enjoying life.

Teachers can create situations to encourage wonder by taking advantage of "teachable moments." This refers to the teacher pausing and making room to explore questions or current events, or to allow time for reflection and research for a "wonder" that has come up in a lesson. These opportunities for responding to wonder honor the learners in the moment by allowing them to use their voices in the learning and providing a two-way learning experience between the teacher and students or student-to-student.

When wonders are shared at an inopportune time, we must have a process in place to capture them. Students can put their thoughts while they are fresh in their minds, on a Wonder Wall, or I've seen a "Parking Lot" chart in classrooms to collect these treasures. If the wonder has been put on pause, it's important to check the Wonder Wall or Parking Lot space, preferably before the class session or day ends to ensure that learners know that their contributions are valuable. Another strategy that can keep the wonders flowing is providing a backchannel for students to use. A backchannel can be as simple as a shared Google Document, or a piece of paper that is at a table where students can write and answer each other's questions during the time of receiving instruction. Students will need support when using a "backchannel" to ensure that the conversations are relevant to the learning.

When my learning management system first came out with the incredible feature to have a streamed conversation, much like those that happen in social media venues, I was eager to share this resource with my students. It was a Friday afternoon, and I helped the students login to practice adding a comment and responding to a classmate's comment. They enjoyed this and it quickly became a wild and silly stream of comments. After modeling what an academic conversation looked like, I explained the expectations for how to use this interactive resource. I felt that the lesson went well and soon our day ended.

Over the weekend, I received a phone call from a parent explaining that I should see what was going on in our online classroom space. The stream of comments started off with what students were eating for breakfast, about a cat that had kittens, and then the comments became inappropriate. Yikes! I turned off the comments with my first reaction to never turn these back on again. Instead, when students arrived Monday morning, I asked them to grab a piece of paper and make two columns. One would have the heading "Academic" and the other would have the heading "Social." Together we looked through each comment (some I had deleted) and put a tally mark in the column that would best describe it. After about ten tally marks in the "Social" column and only two tally marks in the "Academic," we noticed a pattern. I then re-explained the expectation along with my concern for opening up comments again. We brainstormed strategies to make sure that our online conversations were helping our learning, and we tried again, this time with much more success.

Reflecting back on this experience, I look at this differently. I wish that I would have helped the students learn how to use "backchannel" for appropriate Academic and Social conversations, since both are needed. If we are helping a whole person grow and learn, then we need to make time for the true, good, and beautiful to be learned and shared. Social interaction helps us develop our sense of wonder and expands our understanding of facts. Some of my best learning has happened in a social setting, rather than a classroom, and these moments were often really fun. Let your students see you wonder, play, and discover. Imagine the impact that you make on learners, when you answer a question with, "I don't know. Let's research this together."

> Imagine the impact that you make on learners, when you answer a question with, "I don't know. Let's research this together.
>
> ~

The year that I taught two grade levels in a combination class was when I learned to share the load with students and how to provide instruction and resources along a learning continuum. Here's how a few of the lessons played out for me that year:

Learners can be researchers - I invited students to help me do research for questions that were asked and for which we did not have immediate answers.

Learners can be co-designers in lesson planning - My students taught me to shift from recipe lessons to those that incorporated their input. When students are given the learning targets, they can be great partners in finding resources or coming up with ideas to practice and master these goals.

Learners as partners in grading and feedback - In order to provide the curriculum of two grade levels—which when differentiating was actually the curriculum for four or five grade levels, because of remediation and extensions—I learned that not everything needed to be graded by me. I found that students could provide valuable feedback to each other.

Learners as participants in classroom design and function - Out of necessity, due to lack of time, I decided to give empty bulletin boards to my students to put what they thought was important up on the walls. The only requirement was that the items added would need to help them with their learning and they had to explain how the items did just that. This proved to be a success and I found that classroom walls are valuable real estate that really should be populated by student created and chosen artifacts of their learning. Later, when Open House suddenly popped up in October, we didn't have to create anything to display because the classroom walls had become the students' learning gallery. Activating learners and having them contribute is a meaningful resource we can offer them.

Learners using critical thinking and communication - This group of students critiqued my lesson planning and made suggestions for improvement. I had created interactive stations, called SLAM, which stood for Social Studies/Science, Language Arts, and Math, by preparing instruction sheets that included a learning objective, materials/resources, and step-by-step instructions. As students navigated the stations, they gave suggestions for different resources or materials. For example, a student would ask if they had to use the recommended app to record, explaining, "there's a better app for that because it records longer and we have more choices for backgrounds." Over time, the students took over the job of matching a resource to help them accomplish a learning goal. I would observe and give them an opportunity to share why they had chosen a certain resource and they appreciated this. It was like having a shortened version of TED talks happening in our classroom each day.

Learners using collaboration - When reviewing student work, teachers look for common errors in order to adjust instruction as needed. But when teachers are the only ones reviewing for understanding, then learners miss out. I remember sitting at my son's football practice grading a stack of papers and realizing that students would benefit from analyzing and reviewing their own papers more than I would benefit from reviewing the same assignment up to thirty times. I worked with my students to find ways for them to self-check or peer edit for the activities that were happening in SLAM as part of the learning process in the station. This meant less papers were completed, and more analyzing, editing, and revisions on a single paper was happening. The result was deeper learning and I recorded the progress for each student using checklists and rubrics.

Learners develop character and participate in a culture that is learning together - By involving students in the process of learning from the planning, to the doing, and to the sharing, they develop integrity and ownership for their learning. By being a learner myself, I was open to my students' feedback and this became a win for them and for me. I was respectful of my responses to students' feedback knowing that learners stop asking questions when they are fearful of disapproval, embarrassment, or do not feel valued. My job shifted to protecting the valuable resource of wonder and to help them with connecting this to a purpose, goal, and to reflect on the learning that happened because of it.

Learners having fun through creativity and play - How much laughter is heard in your classroom? Laughter is a symptom of having fun and should be a common sound in every learning environment. Learning is hard work and when teachers allow for play, then learners will know that it's OK to experiment and try things out.

When wonder results in play, it is especially memorable. Participating in play is building the foundation for a lifetime of learning. Lev Vygotsky (1978) found that pretend play could be the leading factor in the development of a child's ability to self-regulate. Within play, pretending occurs and this might incorporate point of view, understanding characters, participating in dialogue, problem solving, visualization, sequencing, patterns, divergent thinking, creating scenarios, and making connections. Mr. Fred Rogers reminds us, "Play gives children a chance to practice what they are learning." Play supports growth in executive functioning skills such as organizing, paying attention, understanding points of view, regulating emotions, and self-monitoring. Allowing students to engage in structured and unstructured play will give clues into how they best learn.

Play most likely includes the following: **P**retending, **L**aughter, **A**ction, and **Y**ou.

Pretending

Notice how many skills are being used when pretending. It is ultimately the safest place to make mistakes, which is why simulations are used in various industries.

Laughter

Usually, a surprise or something silly happens during play. Laughter is fun and contagious. Try watching someone laugh without smiling or laughing yourself.

Action

Development and growth can be found in movement, team building, physical skills, higher order thinking, and experimentation. Follow a kid around for a day and you are sure to have a mental and physical work-out!

You

Play helps you regulate your behavior, be goal-directed, and use cognitive skills.

Play can be a driver for innovation. Some of the best academic challenges that prepare students for employment and participation in their community incorporate play. Later we will look at some skill sets that employers seek and innovation is on the list. For now, let's play a bit in our memories.

Think of a time that you invented something from scratch. Was your invention created from your imagination or did you follow some instructions or a recipe? For extra fun, ask your parents or grandparents about a time that they invented something. My grandma shared one of her special childhood memories with me, right around her 89th birthday. I'll try to tell it the way that I remember her sharing:

> *My brother and I were grand inventors when we were children. We loved to experiment with things and make something new out of old things that we found around our house, yard, or neighborhood. One day, our mother gave us a big basket of apples. We used a large pot, chopped up those apples and cooked them for hours. We were so excited about our discovery. The apples had turned to sauce! We poured this sauce into bowls and enjoyed our accomplishment. Weeks later, while at the store, we were shocked to find that someone had stolen our invention. There were cans of applesauce for sale on the store's shelves!*

This was a powerful memory to my grandma and she told me that she thought of this every time she ate applesauce. Think of that; her memory of play and "inventing" applesauce stayed with her for a lifetime. How can we provide experiential learning in our schools? Experimenting is a form of play and in addition to being fun, according to Plato, "You can discover more about one person in a day of play than in a year of conversation."

What keeps us from playing? When you think of the words "childish" or "silly," are these positive or negative in your mind? What about the word "adulting"? Kevin Carroll, author of the book, *Play! Red Rubber Ball Series* (2005) encourages us to play no matter how old we are and explains that playing ball is a universal human experience. Have you had to stop students from engaging in play to keep them on task? While this may be necessary at times, schools need to be infused with opportunities for students to activate their natural resources of wonder and play.

Students come to school with wonder and play as natural resources. These are not items to add to our supply list. We need not worry about only some students having them. We just need to allow space and time for them to be used and shared. Teachers who know how their students best learn, can be the greatest advocates for this to happen.

Learning Spaces

A learning space is wherever people find themselves. The space around us becomes our learning venue, whether we mean for it to or not. When caring for children, our first priority is safety and then providing them with a space to learn on their own, with others, and with guidance.

When my boys were young, there was a time when we didn't have a washer and dryer. Going to the laundromat with a toddler and a 2nd grader proved to be a stressful event. I needed a solution to keep them from running around and from complaining about how long this was taking. On a whim, I put a blanket under the table and a sheet over it, and like magic, there was a fort! The boys climbed in, I handed them some of their books and toys, and they played happily. When I finished the other loads, we threw the blankets and sheets into a washer. I asked the boys to tell me all about their adventure in the fort, while we waited to put this final load in the dryer. It probably helped that they knew we would be walking to the ice cream shop while the last load was drying, but overall, laundry day had been transformed because of a space that was created just for them.

Whether online, blended, hybrid, or in-person, creating flexible learning spaces where students can maximize their learning should be considered a top resource. The article "Australia's Campfires, Caves, and Watering Holes," (2013) by Ann W. Davis and Kim Kappler-Hewitt encouraged me to re-arrange my classroom right after reading it. With help from my students, a few thrift stores, and some imagination, I created the learning spaces of Caves, Campfires, and Watering Holes as described in the article, and added a space called Mountain Top. Look through the following learning spaces and think about where you would best learn when solving a difficult task, creating something new, or reviewing previously learned material. If you're like me, my choice of learning space changes with different tasks. Sometimes I need a quiet space; however, most of the time I prefer a collaborative space. What would each student choose? How might you create flexible learning spaces in response to your students' needs?

A "Cave" learning space provides a quiet area where the learner is able to work without interruptions. I created a classroom "Cave" by using a clear drum shield that I found at a second-hand store, along with an old antique desk, a lamp, and a comfortable padded chair. I put a sign on it calling it the "Recording Studio" because students often used this space to record their own videos. The plexiglass shield provided a sound barrier for the learner, while giving me the ability to see and monitor them. Additional activities that pair well with a "Cave" learning space include: deep thinking, quiet reflection, metacognition, examining your own progress in your learning, making a plan for next steps, and reading, thinking, or wondering. Your classroom "Cave" will be one of your students' favorite places to be. If needed, create more than one space like this. A "Cave" can be instantly created by giving students permission to work under a table or desk. If students are learning online, a "Cave" could be permission to turn off the camera for a little while to think or process. Learning Spaces should be a classroom resource activated by student choice, not as a behavioral consequence.

A "Campfire" learning space provides opportunities to collaborate, network, and problem solve as a team. "Campfires" are great places for design thinking processes, debates, Socratic seminars, and to work collectively on a project or experiment. Students can create a "Campfire" space by simply circling up their chairs or pushing their desks/tables together. They can even circle up and stand to have a "Campfire" chat. One way that I captured "Campfire" discussions and productivity was to have a device propped up to record a video of the action. This was especially helpful when more than one "Campfire" chat was happening at the same time. I was able to fully engage with one group while the others would receive feedback from me after I reviewed their recording. A "Campfire" chat could be a video conference or could take place in a Google document, where the participants are sharing ideas and commenting on one another's suggestions.

"Watering Hole" learning spaces are places to go and fill up with some new knowledge by receiving a lesson or explicit skill instruction. In this space, there is usually a lead speaker (teacher, guest, student) sharing some expertise with the learners. A "Watering Hole" could be a link to a YouTube video, a passage to read, or instructions to follow for an experiment or task. Like each learning space, "Watering Holes" could be set-up for in-person learning or online learning. The "Watering Hole" space is the most familiar in a school setting for getting information to the learners; however, it's important that even in this space, the expectation is two-way communication. I've watched an awesome "Watering Hole" in a construction shop, where students started with the teacher in a classroom setting with tables, chairs, and a whiteboard to go over safety procedures and steps for their projects. Questions were asked and some discussion encouraged at tables to check for understanding before heading out to the shop, where students would be using the equipment and supplies. If students were unable to use safety measures or follow the instructions in the shop, the window in the "Watering Hole" space would serve as a place where they could observe and learn until ready to participate.

"Mountain Top" learning spaces invite students to share what they are learning while the excitement is fresh. Those who best learn in "Mountain Top" spaces will find a way to create them. As a young student, I couldn't wait to share with my classmates, and this hasn't changed. I made "Mountain Tops" by turning around in my seat or talking to someone while walking to get my pencil sharpened, or by passing notes. Some learners need "Mountain Tops" to process the information that they are learning in order for it to stick with them. In an elementary school I visited, I noticed a platform in the front of each of the classrooms. These

platforms or miniature stages were made from recycled wood pallets and plywood. When a learner had something to share, they could step up on the "Mountain Top" and classmates could choose to take a break from what they were doing to listen to the excited speaker. For older students, having them schedule their sharing for a specific date/time on the calendar works well, too. The key to a "Mountain Top" space is to give students an opportunity to choose when they will share their learning.

Involve your students in creating and naming learning spaces and watch for the magic that happens when they are using them.

Bundling Skill Sets

When students understand that learning is their job, that they are not alone in the work of learning, and that they can create, solve problems and share, then learning will be continuous for them. Humans want to make sense of the world around them (True), we need to know that we have something of value to contribute (good), and that our efforts matter (Beautiful) in the present time and in the future. Let's review what a learner's job includes:

Job of a Learner

Listen: I want to learn because of my own curiosity or because I think it is valuable to me.

Empower: I believe in my own abilities to learn.

Analyze: I reflect on what I know, what I hope to learn, or what I've learned.

Resources: I ask for help or know where to find help.

Needs: I understand how I best learn and ask for help when needed.

Experiences: I learn by asking questions, collaborating, investigating, experimenting, creating...

Relationships: I work with others to share my learning or learn from them.

When a student has mastered the *Job of a Learner,* they have prepared themselves for the workplace and have relevant resources to use in life. In addition to required skill sets needed for a specific job description, employers are seeking employees that are critical thinkers, team players, and problem solvers. Employers look for employees to be productive learners who can innovate and communicate.

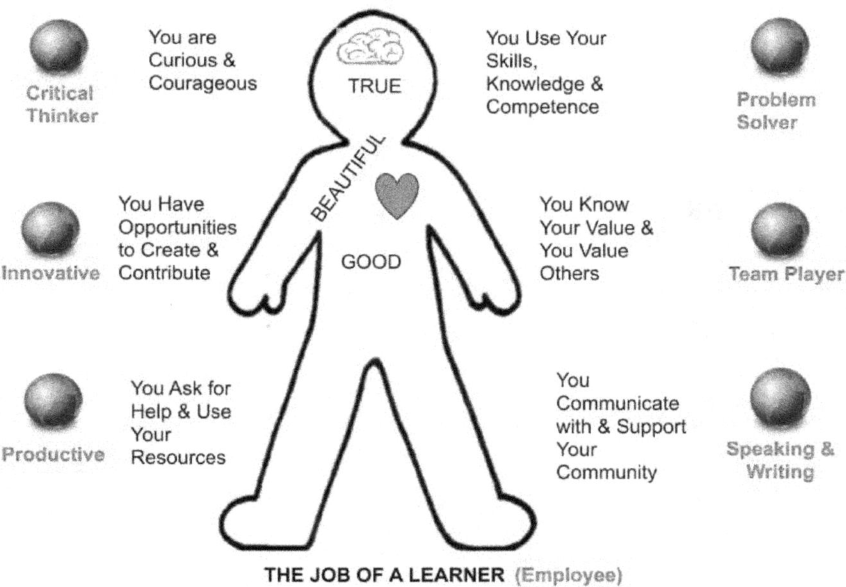

When students make a connection between the knowledge, skills, and personal strengths that they have with what is needed in the workplace or life in general, then success is sure to follow. Help your students see the connection by unpacking their learning. Use the above visual to finish completing the connections between the *Job of a Learner* and, in a general sense, the "Job of an Employee." I've completed the first one with my ideas; add some of your thoughts to the tables below:

Connecting **Job of a Learner** with **Workplace or Life Skills**

LISTEN

I know that I can... Listen and learn because of my own curiosity or because I think that it is valuable to me.

Which helps me be a...critical thinker.

So that I can...accomplish the tasks and learning needed to fulfill my job.

EMPOWER

I know that I can... When I feel **E**mpowered, I believe in my own abilities to learn or I trust my help.

Which helps me be a...team player.

So that I can...____.

ANALYZE

I know that I can...Analyze by reflecting on what I know, what I hope to learn, or what I've learned.

Which helps me be a ...problem solver.

So that I can...____.

RESOURCES

I know that I can...ask for help or I know where to find help by using **R**esources.

Which helps me be a ...productive.

So that I can...____.

NEEDS

I know that I can...understand how I best learn and ask for help when **N**eeded.

Which helps me be a ...learner.

So that I can...____.

EXPERIENCES

I know that I can...participate in **E**xperiences that help me learn by questioning, collaborating, investigating, experimenting, and creating.

Which helps me be...innovative.

So that I can...____.

RELATIONSHIPS

I know that I can...develop **R**elationships by working with others to share my learning or learn from them.

Which helps me be a...

So that I can...______________________________.

Teachers can play matchmaker between a student's interest and a job or community need. Instead of asking students what they want to be when they grow up, help students look at the DNA of jobs that they might be interested in and determine what skills they have or will need to acquire in order to be a candidate for this career choice. Teachers can then give responsive and actionable feedback that will help students develop skills and knowledge to prepare them for career decisions and future educational choices.

Students will benefit from creating learning plans that feature their personal goals and that provide a way to monitor their progress toward these goals. Just like we can connect a specific learning target with an application, learning plans can connect learning targets to develop a learner's expertise. Learners can share their expertise and the skills they have mastered in a learning portfolio right away and on a resume or college application in the future. Learning plans are valuable resources when they incorporate three essential learning processes:

1. *Goals*: K-12 continuum of skill-building and knowledge-developing options that show a student where they are currently working and where they are going next.
2. *Progress:* Relevant assessments and measures of success for each student's K-12 learning growth and development.

3. *Feedback:* Two-way communication (responsive and actionable feedback) between teacher and student to support revision and to make valuable connections to the "Why?" of the learning.

Resources that make a difference, involve the learner. The visual below shows how a Learning Portfolio involves a learner's interest, along with evidence of skills, knowledge, and expertise. Portfolios should feel more like a celebration or "Mountain Top" experience for the learners, rather than an evaluation. Learning Plans curate a learner's goals, progress, and feedback. Learning Plans should feel like a workspace between the learner and those who are supporting them at school and at home. When learning plans are posted and portfolio treasures are highlighted in the school or within the community, this creates a culture of learning and growth. It is important for learning expectations and progress to be transparent for each learner and schools can be fantastic venues for this.

LEARNING PORTFOLIO

MY INTERESTS & EVIDENCE OF SKILLS, KNOWLEDGE, & EXPERTISE

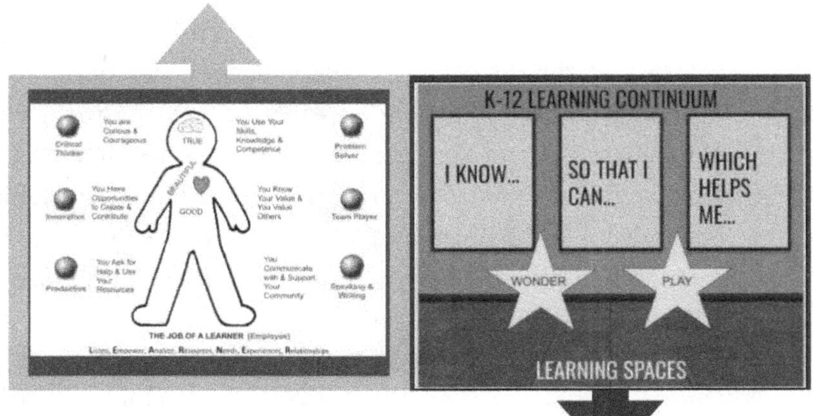

Helping students build bridges between what they learn in school to how they will use their expertise in life, whether this be in college, in a career, or in their homes and communities, should be an ongoing process in K-12 education. Students can bundle their skill sets and curate evidence of their learning through portfolios. Think about a portfolio as a set of playlists. Just like we create playlists for a purpose, such as to inspire us in a workout or relax us before going to sleep, we can help students bundle their skill sets by matching them with a need or purpose. John Hattie, in his book, *Visible Learning for Teachers: Maximizing Impact on Learning,* (2019) encourages educators to involve students in collecting their own evidence of learning and to guide them in monitoring their learning growth. When teachers use helpful resources like portfolios, checklists, and rubrics, they can show students where they are currently at and where they are going next in their learning process. Learning portfolios serve as a place for students to bundle skill sets that they've learned according to their interests and strengths, and potential workplace or life application of these. The following are a few tips to consider when implementing student learning portfolios:

1. *Student Learning Portfolios* are not cumulative files or a student's record that the district or school collects about the student without their input. Portfolios involve students in the curation of their learning and should include what they are interested in.
2. *Student Learning Portfolios* are not a list of classes and credits, but rather a K-12 Learning Continuum written in a way for students to understand where they are in the continuum and where they are headed to next.
3. *Student Learning Portfolios* should include a K-12 Learning Continuum that includes life and workplace skills that reflect community and industry input as to what they are looking for in employees.

4. *Student Learning Portfolios* are not a pacing guide with uniform deadlines that all learners must follow, but rather, real-time learning maps. Portfolios are especially meaningful when students curate their learning evidence of skills, knowledge, and expertise with the assistance of their teachers and families.

Activating student learning plans and portfolios is a way to honor the whole child in their K-12 learning career while helping to prepare learners for future jobs that do not currently exist.

Helping students become master learners will prepare them for any updates and changes that will take place in the future. If those of us in the educational system share the belief that developing and supporting a mindset of learning is an important component of our work and learning growth is the measure of success, then education reform can be happening in real-time; it can be adaptive and responsive to the needs of students, families, and communities.

Activate RESOURCES for Learners

This chapter began with the question, "How Will Learning Continue?" Learning will continue for learners when the True, Good, and Beautiful is involved. Schools and classrooms can integrate all three by providing resources that honor what learners have to offer, by giving them space to learn and develop, and by offering ways to curate and celebrate learning along the way.

Wonder and Play: Check out the following suggestions and pick one or two to try with your students and/or staff.

- Create a Wonder Wall in your classroom for students to add to while their wonders are fresh in their minds.

- Use Question Starters and encourage students to complete these and then research the answers.

- Travel together, even if field trips consist of a neighborhood walk, virtual experiences, or time traveling from your classroom using your imagination.

  Check out the QR Code to visit *Expeditions in Education* for free and fun virtual field trips:

- Share your interests. Create your own TED Talk platform and use it; then share it with your students and other community members, too.

- Research the benefits of Wonder and Play.

- Play ball and games with your students every now and then.

Learning Spaces: Involve students, families, and your community in creating interactive learning spaces. The following suggestions can help guide your conversations and planning.

Learning spaces can be two-dimensional, as well as three-dimensional. Try giving your students the bulletin board and classroom wall spaces to capture evidence of their learning. This will be a time-saver for you, and a rich learning experience for them.

Learning spaces can be online or in-person. Presenting the features of your Learning Management System or use of digital tools as a place and space to learn will be helpful to your students and their families. If your students have many teachers, then calibrate with your colleagues to ensure that you are not creating an overload for them.

Rearrange and create learning spaces with your students. Dream up the plan together, including the purpose for each space and what materials would be awesome. Then look at what you have in your classroom, around the school, or in your homes to build your spaces. Set the expectations together for how these spaces will be used and shared.

Bundling Skills Sets:
Incorporate Student Learning Plans and Portfolios to support students in doing their Job as Learners and to curate evidence that education is

a service to them. Spend time with your students, families, and your community to review the following questions and ideas:

- What is our K-12 continuum of skill building and knowledge developing options that show a student where they are currently working and where they are going next?
- Do the K-12 learning experiences connect with needed workplace or life skills?
- How do we support two-way communication (responsive & actionable feedback) between teachers and students to support revision and to make valuable connections to the "Why" for the learning?
- What are some examples of relevant assessments and measures of success that capture each student's K-12 learning growth and development?

Finding the True, Good, and Beautiful

A learning plan and learning portfolio combination that incorporates the True, Good, and Beautiful (as listed in the table below) serves both the student and the system of education. For the student, they can monitor their current progress and curate evidence of their strengths and competencies that could populate a resume' in their future. For the education system, analyzing student learning plans and portfolios can take the place of measurements that tend to lose an individual's learning success.

True	**Good**	**Beautiful**
Essential Competencies/ Standards	Connections/ Collaboration	Strengths/Interests
Goals/Measures of Success Each student's learning goals and plans are essential and appropriate for them (meeting them where they are). Portfolios curate learning progress for each student.	*Communication/ Feedback* Each student's learning plan provides a space for two-way communication, feedback, and support. Each student's learning goals and plans provide ways for students to apply their learning at home, school, and in their community.	*Evidence/ Connections* Learning goals are valuable to each student by connecting to interests and strengths. Portfolios can be used to bundle skill sets that the learner has mastered with what is needed in their community and the world.

CHAPTER 5

Needs: What Will Support Learners?

Listen, Empower, Analyze, Resources, ***Needs,*** *Experiences, Relationships*

"Never discourage anyone who continually makes progress, no matter how slow."
Plato

An *Oath for Learners* has helped us tackle the following questions so far:

Listen - Where is your attention?
Empower - Who is learning?
Analyze - What is learning?
Resources - How will learning continue?

As we look at **Needs** in this chapter, we have the guiding question, what will support learners? You are the best support to the learners you serve, when you are healthy, whole, and your needs are met. Take some time to do your own learning check-up to see how much hope that you have for where you are right now, determine if you have basic needs that require support, and if you are learning.

A Note to Teachers:

Thank you for wearing the many hats that it takes to care for your students. Please take care of yourself in the same way that you love and care for others around you. Your health, feelings, and interests are important. Are there things that you are doing *for* your students, colleagues, and families that they would benefit from doing *with* you? Take a few days to write down how you spend your time and mark the items that filled you up and those that drained you down. If you have more items that drain you, reach out to a colleague or friend to brainstorm ways to flip this. It may be one of the biggest challenges for you to secure your own seatbelt and use your own oxygen mask before helping others, but this is essential and ultimately helps your students as well. Take a look at the *Job of a Learner* and see how you are doing when you put yourself as the learner:

The Job of a Learner

Listen: I want to learn because of my own curiosity or because I think it is valuable to me.

Empower: I believe in my own abilities to learn.

Analyze: I reflect on what I know, what I hope to learn, or what I've learned.

Resources: I ask for help or know where to find help.

Needs: I understand how I best learn and ask for help when needed.

Experiences: I learn by asking questions, collaborating, investigating, experimenting, and creating.

Relationships: I work with others to share my learning or learn from them.

When you are filled with hope, you can offer hope to others. Learners help learners, and hope is a prerequisite for learning. While this work takes time and progress can seem slow, never forget helping learners find hope is life-changing and deeply rewarding. It is worth your time.

Hope is a Prerequisite for Learning

"Please start by putting your name on the paper and then I will come help you with the next step," I explained as I looked into the eyes of Cody, a young student who struggled with self-starting. This was the deal that we had made together; however, there were times that he didn't want to keep his end of the bargain. I worked to be consistent with my response of softly reminding him of our deal, and then giving him some space to try again. Sometimes he would write his name quickly on his paper and then harmoniously seek me out for the next step, other times he wouldn't. I thought about changing my approach on the day he sat at his table screaming C-O-D-Y as he scribbled his name violently at the top of his paper. I wanted Cody to believe that he could begin on a project or assignment alone, even if it was just getting his name on the paper before asking for help. Each time he took this first step, I followed up with my promise to be there to help him with the next one. A month passed before Cody consistently self-started by writing his name on the paper and he was taking the next steps for the project or assignment to the best of his ability. A win for Cody in the classroom, but it wasn't until our Fall Fun Run that I realized that this was really a win for Cody in life.

The Fall Fun Run was an annual event at our school where students and teachers took turns running a mile around the field. On the morning of the race, I explained to my students that I wasn't feeling very good and didn't know if I should participate. Some students groaned with disappointment and others nodded their heads with understanding. When the bell rang to go out, I put on my running shoes and decided to give the race a try. At the half-mile mark, I was really struggling; my body and will were starting to give up and my pace slowed to a fast walk. I heard my students cheering me on and I felt a small hand grab my left arm. Cody was holding on and jogging next to me. I looked into his determined eyes, smiled, and picked up my pace. He let go and was running to keep up and shouting, "Mrs. D. don't worry, I'm not going to leave you. You can do this. Keep running, I believe in you." We reached the final lap and Cody fell behind me; he had lost his shoe. Just as I reached the finish, he caught up to me with one shoe in his hand, one shoe on his foot and the greatest smile on his face as we crossed the line together. We could hear kids, teachers, and families cheering us on in the background, but the beautiful words that I have forever in my heart were the loudest, as Cody hugged me and said, "I knew you could do it. And you did, Mrs. D." It was then that I knew that Cody was going to be OK, for not only had he discovered hope, he knew how to share hope.

Hope is a universal human need that brings a promise of the future or the understanding that help is on the way. Having hope requires action on our part, the willingness to trust the person, promise, and/or process. C.R. Snyder's work on Hope Theory shared in his book, *The Psychology of Hope*, (2010) explains that we experience hope based on our "Will Power" and "Way Power." Snyder refers to these key factors as Pathways Thinking (Way Power) and Agency Thinking (Will Power) and explains how they both influence a person's growth toward achievement of goals. In Cody's situation, he needed to see a **way**, before he could have a **will** to start. Upon having success, even if this was getting his name on the paper, he would demonstrate the **will** to try the next step. When learners have a **will** to learn, they are open to receiving instruction or taking action, which is where they will find a **way** for the next needed step.

Can you find Pathways Thinking and Agency Thinking, or a **will** and **way** in the following excerpt from the movie *Apollo 13* (1995)? Gene Kranz, the Flight Director listens to a conversation between two

NASA directors as they discuss the dismal situation that the broken spacecraft is in. This is what Kranz hears: "I know what the problems are Henry." One of them explains, "This could be the worst disaster NASA has ever experienced." Flight Director Kranz interrupts with a different perspective and says, "With all due respect, Sir, I believe this is going to be our finest hour." Hope is a prerequisite for learning and it is driven by thoughts prior to action.

> Hope is a prerequisite for learning and it is driven by thoughts prior to action.
>
> 

The following visual shows how C.R. Snyder's Framework of Goals, Agency, and Pathways can be found in the *Job of a Learner*. Goal setting involves a learner's use of skills, knowledge, or competence, along with their curiosity and courageousness to make a plan to begin with. While learner "Agency" (the **will** or choice) can be activated through opportunities for them to create and contribute, their belief in their own capacity and knowing their value is a motivating factor for their participation. When learners know what support is available to them, and how to ask for help, then they can see the "Pathways" (the **way**) to their success. This is where learners can see step-by-step the ways in which to move in order to reach their goal.

Education can be a service that provides hope to students and their families. When a student is not making progress, figure out why they have lost their **will** and help them find a **way** forward. Gather a team to circle the student with support, at school and at home. I had an opportunity to see this in action during a high school student's Individualized Education Plan (IEP) annual review. At first the team started by listing the issues and challenges that the student was having at school and at home. Then the teacher shared some of the student's strengths and encouraged us to think about how to use these to support the student's learning goals. She further explained that the student's negative

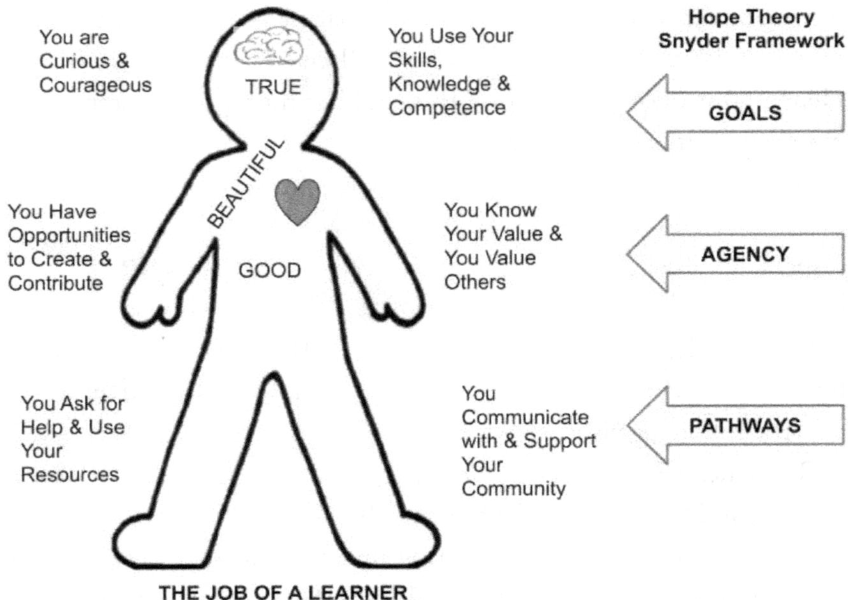

Listen, **E**mpower, **A**nalyze, **R**esources, **N**eeds, **E**xperiences, **R**elationships

behavior was evidence that we had not yet found a way to help the learner. The parent spoke with a soft voice and through tears, to share that out of many IEP meetings, this was the first time that she felt her child was seen and understood. She thanked the team and explained that if her child felt the hope that she was feeling, she knew that success would come.

Inspiring teachers support learners with the vision, or "hope," for success. When I taught kindergarten, I called my students, "readers." Some students would challenge me on this and say, "Teacher, I can't read." I would ask if they knew any letters, and they would share the ones they knew. Then I'd show them a picture in a book and ask what they noticed. After they explained their observations, I would say, "You see, you are a reader." They had skills that were leading up to the process of reading, maybe they hadn't reached the goal that they had for themselves, but they were on their way. Before you became a reader, there might have been someone calling you a reader. Or before you were a teacher, someone might have called you a teacher. Having someone help us see our skills and how these can pave a way for our future is what we need.

Does our education system allow for each person to be seen and loved in order to help them develop their full potential? When looking at our K-12 system, where does the rate of learning dip the most? For many this happens in middle school or junior high. Judy Willis, a neuroscientist and teacher, explains in a "Science of Learning" video (2011) that learning only occurs when a person is thinking. And with our understanding of hope, we could say that only a person who hopes, learns. Willis' work highlights a growth spurt that happens between the ages of 8 and 16 in the development of the prefrontal cortex. This is the area that allows for executive functioning skills.

Middle school/junior high is also when our education system shifts from a focus of developmental learning to content-focused learning. Are students losing hope as learners because the education system is based on a calendar and time that doesn't align with their needs, abilities, and developmental progress? Plato's wisdom warns us to "Never discourage anyone who continually makes progress, no matter how slow." If the content taught at this age-level aligned with the development of the brain to highlight executive functioning skills, such as problem solving, critical analysis, evaluation, risk assessment, and long-term planning, this would serve students throughout their lifetime.

Although having hope and making the decision to learn is personal, when facing challenges, we need each other to thrive. The same goal can be in front of two people; however, the decision to begin, try, and persevere is up to each individual. As I shared earlier, both my husband and I had the same goal to climb Mt. Borah. We spent time together thinking about what was possible. Then, we made a choice together to pack the truck and drive to the trailhead. As we planned the trip, I imagined myself reaching the summit and planned how I might celebrate.

I can still hear my husband's voice as we stood at the base of Chicken Out Ridge, the rugged scramble that we faced before the final ascent to the summit: "We are going to summit this mountain today." I thought, "How strange; of course we are!" since my decision for reaching that goal had already been confirmed when I put my headlamp on and tied my boots at 4:00 a.m. You see, we each had to arrive at our own decision to do it. Having it on the calendar, having all of the resources for our needs, and the ability to walk helped make this possible, but we each needed to decide to put one foot in front of the other.

Schools can triage support for students by using the true, good, and beautiful to ensure that all learners are reminded of their value and that they are supported in finding a way to move forward. We can help our students, their families, our co-workers, and our community members find hope by helping them find another option when they feel stuck or overwhelmed (true), by reminding them that help is available (good), and by giving them space to activate their strengths in order to take the next step (beautiful).

How about Breakfast?

In addition to hope as a basic need, we can look to Maslow's Hierarchy of Needs (1943) to ensure that students are ready for learning. Living in the era of COVID-19, where at-home video conferences became our learning venues, I have a better understanding of the challenges that students, parents, co-workers, and community members are experiencing. Take a few minutes to write down what has changed for you and those you care for since the beginning of this global challenge. What do you know now about your school community needs that you didn't know before? What adjustments are being made or do you hope will be made to meet these needs?

We know that physical variables such as nutrition, sleep, and exercise affect how and if we can learn. The environment including space, temperature, lighting, and even furniture can affect learning success as well. When a learner is safe and cared for they are more willing to try something new or share their learning with someone. Think of a small child sitting at the top of a tall slide. What are they thinking when they look down? If they have a loved one waiting for them at the bottom, chances are they have a giant smile on their face and they push off and squeal with joy all the way down. If this is the child's first time down a slide, or if they are hungry, tired, or have had a scary slide experience in the past, then they might look down in horror and become frozen in fear. At this point, scaffolding comes into place with the adult asking the child if they would like to sit on their lap to slide down, or they might hold the little buddy's hand while they help them swoop down. The goal is to successfully make it down the slide and then confidence comes. You know that you are making progress with the slide experience when the child says, "Again!" Mastery leads to confidence. Confidence encourages our curiosity and then we want to explore, discover, and, yes, go "Again!"

When a student feels that safety, care, or connection is missing in their classroom or school, the result can be a lost and discouraged learner.

Learners seek more learning when they are experiencing success. Having an "Aha" moment is a basic need in the learning process because small wins lead to big wins. When a learner has a memory of an "Aha," they will push through difficult challenges and care about their progress. When a student feels that safety, care, or connection is missing in their classroom or school, the result can be a lost and discouraged learner.

Has there been a time when you felt discouraged and not supported in your learning? I have a vivid memory of this kind of experience from junior high school. Sitting in seventh grade Pre-Algebra class was awful. First, I didn't know how solving equations and memorizing formulas would be helpful to me at that moment or in the future. Second, I felt uncomfortable sitting in the rigid desk in that classroom, facing forward, and with no talking allowed. Finally, I felt embarrassed that I didn't understand a word that Mr. DeNali was saying during his lesson lecture. My strategies for finding some success in this class included looking at my friend's paper, using the even answers in the back of the math book to get at least half of my homework correct, and not letting anyone know that I didn't understand how to solve the math problems. When I was brave enough to leave my desk and walk up the aisle to Mr. Denali's desk to ask for help, his repeated instructions didn't provide clarity.

On a particular test day, my lack of skills became transparent when I had no idea how to work most of the problems on the page. While I was turning around from my desk, getting some help from a friend's paper, Mr. DeNali passed through the aisle and said, "Marita, I have my eye on you." Giggles and gasps were heard from around the room, as I whipped around in my chair to face forward, and to discover that Mr. DeNali had removed his glass eye and placed it on my desk in the space that held pencils. I was horrified and terribly embarrassed. I never turned around in my chair again for the rest of the semester. Somehow, I managed to get a B on my report card. The strategies that Mr. DeNali used to stop me from cheating in math class, actually became barriers to my learning due to fear, embarrassment, and self-doubt that kept me from the desire or belief that I could learn in Pre-Algebra class.

Fast forward years later, I was sitting in a testing room taking the Graduate Record Examination, or GRE, and although I had developed skills to solve many of the algebra problems in front of me, I was experiencing anxiety as time counted down. When the testing proctor reached over me to place some scratch paper in my testing cubicle, I had a flashback of Mr. DeNali's glass eye and all logic went out the window for at least five minutes. When learners lack understanding for the expected learning experiences, they can feel like something is wrong with them, and this can put them in fight, flight, or freeze mode when facing similar content or learning experiences well into their future.

Our greatest struggles can become a gift to someone else. My traumatic math experience helped me empathize with Elena, a student who experienced math anxiety to an extreme. She developed a habit of pulling her hair out when working on math problems that she didn't understand. According to her school file, she had been doing this on and off for a few years. There were instructional supports in place to help Elena with math concepts and modifications to her assignments, however, I understood that this was bigger than math. This was about Elena not wanting to let others know that she didn't understand something and she was hard on herself when she didn't master something quickly. She struggled with learning, in general.

Upon analyzing the whole situation, I had a conference with Elena and let her know that I was going to help her learn math when she was ready. Then I gave her permission to do something that she really enjoyed instead of math. I explained how I used to be a cosmetologist and that I recognized and appreciated beautiful hair and couldn't bear the thought that she would pull any of her hair out just because of math. Therefore, we decided to take math out of the equation for Elena for at least two weeks.

As a teacher feeling the need to get through the content, I worried that Elena would fall behind in math. But as a learner who experienced math anxiety, I knew that until she could discover why math was important to her and see that she had support to understand how math worked, she would not be making gains. One week went by and while math stations were happening, Elena would be reading, writing, or drawing. On the Friday of the first week, she said, "I think that I should be doing math." I asked if she was sure about this and asked her to explain why learning math was important to her. She explained, "All week, I've still been doing math. I've been listening to you teach in stations and I've been doing this in my notebook." Sure enough, her math notes were sketches! We both discovered Elena could connect the math concepts to visuals in a unique way. I helped Elena connect her love of **beautiful** art with **true** knowledge of mathematics and she became a successful learner in this subject.

Just like we provide breakfast to students when they arrive at school hungry, we must provide understanding and care when students arrive to class discouraged. We can start by asking the question, "How are you feeling?" Keeping lines of communication open with our students and meeting them where they are to provide needed instruction and feedback are important ways to help them in their continued learning.

Learning to Learn

Me: When did you start learning? Did this happen when you were a baby or when you started preschool?

My Four-Year-Old Granddaughter: Well, babies learn. You just need to let newborns do their thing.

Me: What is their "thing"?

My Four-Year-Old Granddaughter: Learning how to learn.

College and career readiness is a common topic in education shared in discussions, conferences, keynotes, and other K-12 professional development opportunities. I remember attending a session on this topic, along with high school teachers, high school college and career advisors, principals, and district superintendents that ended in a surprise. The speaker served at a community college where they had recently launched a class for college freshmen, that would help the students learn how they learn. As the conversation continued, I became more uncomfortable. I wondered why students needed to take a college course to help them learn how to learn, after finishing their K-12 education experience. As my granddaughter explained, learning is the "thing" that we all do as humans, from the time we are born. It is important for students to learn how they best learn at a young age, as this will help them be advocates for their learning needs.

Are the best students truly the best learners? Measures of K-12 education success need to incorporate the expectation that students know how they best learn, students know how to use resources, and students know how to advocate for help, when needed.

Learners need to believe that they can learn. There is a myth about learning that has been busted. You don't have a math brain, reading brain, or music brain; instead, you have a brain that has the capability to learn. I've heard parents link their child's learning struggle with their own, making statements like, "My daughter is taking after me, because I am terrible at math." Environments nurture mindsets that can be helpful or harmful to the process of learning; however, according to K. Anders Ericsson's 30-year research shared in his book, *Peak: Secrets from the New Science of Expertise* (2017), all can adapt and learn when provided with training and practice. All *can* learn; however, there is another element to consider. Does someone *want* to learn?

When attaching personal value or identity to the success of learning, then learning can be stifled. Students might not feel safe to explain that they don't understand something, when according to their grade level expectations, they "should" know something. Ranking and sorting students according to their achievement or their age takes the focus off the learning and the learner. Learning is fueled by curiosity and joy, not statistical benchmarks.

Learners need guidance and space. Learning requires hope, risk-taking, admission of not knowing, reflecting on failure, and perseverance. My two sons, five and a half years apart and the best of friends, experienced many adventures together in which my oldest son was the teacher and my youngest son was the student. When my youngest son turned four years old, his older brother was sure that it was time for him to learn how to ride his bike without training wheels; after all, that was how old he had been when he learned how to ride a bike. As both seemed to be in agreement, I helped remove the training wheels from the bike and off they went to begin bike riding lessons out on our long gravel driveway. I hovered for a bit, giving suggestions and encouragement, and then my nine-year-old let me know that this was a "brother thing." I smiled and walked into the house to watch from the window. After many falls, some tears, and disappointment, my youngest came barreling into the front door and yelled, "Mom, I'm not a bike rider, I'm a roller blader!" I helped him clean up and explained that it takes time to learn and encouraged him not to give up.

Weeks went by and his bike stayed in the shed. Then one day, while my oldest son was at school, my little guy said, "Mom, I want to take my bike out and wash it." I helped him get out supplies and he scrubbed down his bike. It sat there shiny in the driveway with a kickstand holding it up. As I was doing some chores around the house, I peered out the window and noticed that he had put his helmet on and was out in the driveway by himself with his bike. It didn't take long and he was a bike rider. Learning doesn't always happen according to someone else's goals or timelines. Sometimes a teacher can create a situation that motivates a learner to make a goal, and sometimes a teacher needs to give some time and space for the learner to decide that they are ready to learn. Ultimately, it is the learner's goals and timelines that are the driver and then a teacher can be the accelerator. There needs to be a desire to learn before the learning can happen.

Ultimately, it is the learner's goals and timelines that are the driver and then a teacher can be the accelerator.

Learners need relevant and personal feedback. Does the way that we grade learning encourage our students to continue learning? Todd Rose explains in his book, *The End of Average* (2015), that the idea of average doesn't exist. When we create an average using mathematics, how many people are represented with that number? Calculating averages for grades can be just as deceiving. I remember pleading with my students to turn in something rather than nothing because our school had the practice of giving zeros to missing work. I did the simple math to show them that if they had three equally weighted assignments, two of which were 100% and one was 0%, then their average grade, that I was expected to put on a report card, would be a 66.7%, a barely passing grade of D. Not a fair or correct representation of their learning. As I continued to wonder and research about this, I realized that averaging was not a fair or correct way to calculate grades. What artificial benchmarks have been created within our K-12 system that have caused damage to our students, under the assumption that there is such a thing as average?

While averages and benchmarks can be used to see if there are patterns or themes showing progress in an overall system, they are problematic and unfair when used to define an individual learner. I have a memory of my son coming home from middle school to tell me that he had made a goal to increase his standardized test score by ten points. I asked him how he arrived at this goal. He explained that his teacher asked him to make a goal and all of his friends had ten points for their goals. What he didn't have control over was a guarantee that he would be given learning opportunities that would help him reach his goal. Helping learners make goals and accomplish them is a critical part of their education; however, this requires relevant instruction, resources, and feedback to help learners monitor their learning progress. Schools need to offer opportunities that support learners to grow from where they are, rather than engaging them in unhealthy or inequitable competition.

The system of K-12 education should be set up as a learning progression for students to set goals and record milestones. If these learning progressions stayed with the student, much like a medical record does, regardless of your provider, they could have continual learning without starts and stops. Think about how many times you reviewed the same concepts at the beginning of each grade level. How much more could you have learned if you were able to pick up where you left off before summer break? When a K-12 system is set up in this way, it allows the opportunity for educators to support learners until they master a concept or skill, rather than moving them on because of their age or the calendar month.

Learners need choices and strategies. The book, *Learning How to Learn,* (2018) by Barbara Oakley and Terrence Sejnowski, gives information about how learning works from a brain perspective. This team has also partnered with Arizona State University to provide a video series geared for students to help them understand that learning happens when a brain goes back and forth between focused mode and diffused mode. Focused mode incorporates thinking that you've done before; it is familiar, and you already have a pathway that helps you look at details. Diffused mode is where you are thinking about something for the first time or in a completely different way. This is where innovation lives, where you can look at the big picture. My takeaways from this work align with what I know as a learner and as a teacher. Every learner has unique strengths and challenges, along with different experiences, which means that every learner will move in and out of focused mode and diffused mode in their own way. How can we help learners make progress in both modes of thinking?

Francesco Cirillo's *Pomodoro Technique* (2018) is one strategy to try. This is where a learner decides what task they would like to accomplish, finds a place to focus on the work without interruptions, sets a timer for about 25 minutes, and then allows for a 5-10 minute break as a reward. The sense of accomplishment isn't the only thing that you gain from this strategy, you have given your brain an opportunity to activate both the focused and diffused mode to accomplish your task. How does your school or district allow for spaced intervals of learning? If this is done at the same time for the same task with every student, you have probably noticed that it's working for some and not others.

Learners need encouragement and challenges. How can we help a learner who appears to be stuck? Even at a young age, learners will check to see if they have reliable help available to them. My two-year-old grandson will purposely fall to the ground, lie on his back, hold up his hands, and say, "I stuck." A loved one will pass his test by either reaching out to help him up or by offering him a strategy to help himself up. Encouragement is a need for learners, because learning can be painful and disheartening. Learning something new is difficult and when we feel that we need to be at a certain place at a certain time, it adds to the natural cognitive conflict that takes place. I remember one of my students described learning as feeling sick to her stomach.

Have you ever felt queasy when taking on a new or difficult task? Sometimes we fight the process of learning and get angry or impatient with ourselves when learning something new. Jean Piaget's theory of cognitive development (1971) referred to this as a state of cognitive imbalance or cognitive disequilibrium. Brains do not like to be in disequilibrium; the experience is not familiar and, therefore, we feel uncomfortable. Dr. Judy Willis (2016), explains how when a learner is experiencing stress, the only behavior that results is fight, flight, or freeze. She further explains how boredom can create stress and offers a strategy to combat this by comparing a classroom model with a video game.

My sons introduced me to the world of video games when they were younger. At times they would ask me to join them, but I didn't play at their level. While I was happy to move from Level 1 to Level 2, they shared a goal of beating the game. Willis (2016) explains that while everyone enters the game at Level 1, each person has their "achievable challenge level." My sons would reach higher levels due to the time spent in trial and error, collaborating about techniques with friends, and ultimately they were more curious than I was about the game. Willis' "achievable challenge level" relates to the work of Vygotsky's Zone of Proximal Development, (1978) where students can either accomplish the learning target independently or with some guidance. Video games allow learners to see what is happening from their effort and they can receive corrective feedback, when they want it. In games, the reward for accomplishing a level is harder work, the next level.

Learners need true, good, and beautiful learning opportunities. Teachers can help students discover their "achievable challenge level" by providing multisensory learning experiences that are enriching for their students' brains. Willis offers the acronym RAD (**R**eticular activating system, **A**mygdala, **D**opamine) to help teachers incorporate three neuroscience concepts into learning opportunities. Willis' article, "The Neuroscience of Joyful Education" (2007, p.9) unpacks the acronym this way:

> Novelty promotes information transmission through the **R**eticular activating system.
>
> Stress-free classrooms propel data through the **A**mygdala's effective filter.
>
> Pleasurable associations linked with learning are more likely to release more **D**opamine.

In what ways can you activate RAD learning in your school or district? Let's give some attention to each of the concepts and imagine them in action.

If you are looking for ways to bring novelty into learning experiences, you are sure to find treasure with Dave Burgess' book, *Teach Like a Pirate* (2018). Burgess is a master at hooking learners through surprise, wonder, and great fun. You will find many ideas to encourage student engagement, but remember you are the best gift for your students. If you are having fun and learning, then most likely your students will, too.

How can schools and classrooms create a stress-free learning environment? In addition to providing the "achievable challenge level," students need to experience choice. Learners need to think about what they need in order to learn and what can help them power through a difficult task. Sometimes the need is a different space to learn.

Pleasurable associations linked with learning, or joyful learning experiences, stick with us; they become memories that we carry with us long after the initial learning took place. What makes a learning experience pleasurable? What is it about a day that makes it good? Chip and Dan Heath's research provides an answer. In their book, *Power of Moments,* (2019) they explain that moments are memorable when they fall into these four categories: connection, insight, elevation, and pride. When learners are actively involved in their learning, they are able to develop self-insight and advocate for their needs. Teachers can encourage this in learners, asking them to reflect by making true, good, and beautiful connections to the content that they are learning.

When I think about a good day, it is one when I felt loved and was able to love someone else (connection), when I learned something new (insight), and when I contributed using my unique skills and talents (elevation/pride). Do you see a true, good, and beautiful connection with these four elements?

Insight - True
Connection - Good
Elevation, Pride - Beautiful

As educators, we can create memorable moments for our students by incorporating these elements that are sure to help our students do their amazing "thing" of learning how to learn.

Activate NEEDS for Learners

This chapter focused on learning needs and asked the question, "What Will Support Learners?" Learners who have hope, who have their basic and learning needs met, and autonomy to learn how they best learn are sure to see achievement of goals and continuous growth. Teachers provide the best support when they are caring for themselves as learners, too. As an education service, we need to focus on each learner's continual progress.

Hope is a Prerequisite for Learning:
Help students see a **way** to learn, and you will notice that their **will** follows. Here are some ideas:

- Help students see why the learning target is a priority and how it is valuable to them.
- Break up the goal into small parts. Provide support for each part.
- Celebrate small wins along the way. Once they have something mastered, give them an opportunity to teach and share their new skill(s).
- Listen, empower, analyze, and connect students to resources that will help them with next steps. Give them responsive and actionable feedback with scaffolding as needed.
- Let goal setting and goal achievement be an enjoyable process. Be aware of making comparisons between learners or putting students into unfair competitions, as these can stifle the enjoyment of learning.
- When none of your strategies work, seek additional help. The student's lack of hope could be a symptom of a need that requires immediate support.

What's for Breakfast?

Spend some time thinking about your students. What are their strengths and their struggles? Is there a student or two that you don't know well? Take time to have a conversation on a weekly basis until you do.

The Yale Center for Emotional Intelligence (2020) has resources to help people understand the value of emotions while supporting them in building skills of emotional intelligence.

Check out resources such as the Mood Meter and RULER acronym, here:

Spend some time thinking about how you are doing. The resources and strategies that you share with your students can work for you, too. How are you caring for yourself? Make time to be where you rest and recharge the best. Start your day with a good breakfast and ask yourself how you are doing throughout the day. You matter.

Learning To Learn:

The following questions can be revisited. For now, choose one and run with it:

- What is the achievable challenge level for each student on the specific expected learning target?
- How can students be supported through flexible grouping?
- How is learning the reward?
- Are extrinsic rewards numbing the "Aha!" moments, the natural intrinsic motivation that gets the dopamine level up?

- What timely and corrective feedback is available to students while they are learning?
- In what ways is personal responsibility encouraged?
- Do your students know why they are learning and how they learn best?

Finding the True, Good, and Beautiful

When we know how our students learn best and how to support them when learning is difficult, we involve them in the learning process and the impact is long-lasting. Review the following questions in the True, Good, and Beautiful table below and create some of your own questions by reflecting on ways that you feel supported when learning and how you support others.

True	**Good**	**Beautiful**
Learning is enjoyable to me when...	I enjoy sharing my learning with others by...	I am happiest in my learning when I can...
Learners need...	Learners share...	Learners can create...
I Know...	So That I Can...	Which Helps Me...

CHAPTER 6

Experiences: What is Valuable to Learners?

Listen, Empower, Analyze, Resources, Needs, ***Experiences,*** *Relationships*

"Human Behavior flows from three main sources: desire, emotion, and knowledge."
Plato

Learning experiences should be designed to enhance or edit a learner's knowledge and skills. Ultimately, this means that behavior adapts or changes. Plato's quote explains how "desire, emotion, and knowledge" all need to be considered when looking to change behavior. Do you see the True, Good, and Beautiful? Notice how we are five steps into the *The Oath for Learners,* "to **listen** to and **empower** my students to develop their full potential. I will **analyze** and study my students. I'll help provide hope to my students by matching **resources** to their **needs**," prior to designing "**experiences** that support each student's growth." If teachers go through these five steps before lesson planning, they have the information needed to answer the question, "What is valuable to the learners I serve?" In the same way that a new paint job is better when the appropriate prep work has been done and needed materials have been collected, so are the learning experiences better when they have been customized for learners.

Responsive teachers work hard to create **experiences** that will help students learn academically and develop socially. The shift to remote or blended learning during the COVID-19 Pandemic added onto the challenge of creating personalized learning experiences for students. Many teachers, students, and families have been learning how to connect without being together in person; some are using digital tools and cloud-based computing for the first time. While many school systems have worked to ensure that students have connectivity and devices to access the Internet from home, hard-working teachers have been striving to offer learning experiences that are meaningful and supportive. Changes to the way that instruction is being delivered and received has required digital citizenship skills along with new technical skills. Although these changes and learning experiences have been difficult to navigate, they have provided evidence that many educators are seeking to answer the question, "What is valuable to learners?"

This chapter focuses on **Experiences**, incorporating the true, good, and beautiful into learning experiences and can be a guide for educators as they continue to adapt in order to provide equity, relevance, and responsiveness to help their students. Regardless of the learning venue, learning experiences are most valuable when they offer opportunities to make mistakes (true), to receive and give feedback (good), and to innovate or establish valuable connections (beautiful).

Oops!

Learning experiences need to include room for students to make mistakes, reflect, exhibit perseverance, and adapt. An "Oops!" delivers an opportunity for teachers to provide feedback that is both responsive to the situation and actionable in helping learners modify and adjust before trying again.

Experiences That Require Safety and Scaffolding. When I was in cosmetology school, many of my learning experiences happened in a safe space in terms of making errors. The stakes were low, as all the haircuts, colors, and perms were done on a mannequin. I developed techniques, my instructor provided feedback, and soon I was ready to provide services to actual people.

I'll never forget the first time that I did an eyebrow waxing. I greeted my new client, a kind elderly lady with extremely bushy eyebrows, at the door of the school. We talked about the weather as I helped her lean back in the reclining chair and set her up for the procedure. Her eyebrows grew in many directions and required multiple attempts of applying wax, then patting and pulling using strips of muslin cloth. Upon completing one eyebrow, I could tell that my sweet client was uncomfortable, so I decided to try a different strategy on the other.

For the next side, I gobbed the wax on and attached a large strip of cloth to hopefully get the bulk of the hair in the first attempt. I told her that we'd go quick on this side and then gave a strong pull. My client who was laying there with cotton balls over her eyes exclaimed, "Ooh, that one stung a bit." I apologized and started to give her a gentle face massage while looking over her and staring in horror at half of the eyebrow that remained. I had taken the other half off on the muslin cloth. I scanned the room, made eye contact with my instructor, and waved her over. She took a look at what I had just done, then quickly walked away and returned with an eyebrow pencil. We had a silent conversation and then I applied the eyebrow pencil to my client's eye and explained that the wax took more than I had expected. My client was gracious to me; as I held back tears she said, "Don't worry honey, it will grow back." I helped her sit up, handed her the pencil, and walked her out the door, profusely apologizing. My "Oops!" left more than a sting; it left a lasting impact on another person. I had needed more instruction. It would have been helpful if my instructor modeled the process for one eyebrow, and then provided guidance, as I did the other. When errors can be damaging or dangerous, then more scaffolding is needed during learning experiences and mastering such skills is essential.

Experiences with Peer Feedback. Depending on the content and level of safety required, we can involve students in the process of providing responsive and actionable feedback to their peers. I remember watching a small group of students huddled around the whiteboard in my classroom, working together to solve a multi-step math problem. Esther was explaining her process through the problem using the large whiteboard, while the others used their individual whiteboards or papers. When she finished, another student spoke up and said, "Esther, I respectfully disagree with your answer. You made an addition mistake." Esther looked over her work, found the error, fixed it, and then proceeded to rework the problem from there. Esther's mom, who was volunteering in class that morning, walked over to her after she sat down and whispered loud enough for the room to hear, "Oh Esther, you must be so embarrassed. I'm so sorry." Esther looked at her mom confused.

The idea of "respectfully disagreeing" was an expected practice in our classroom; however, I realized that I had left out an important group of people—our parents and volunteers—when we established this workflow that was based on our *Class Constitution*. This document was written as a team during the first week of school, after playing a "Game with No Rules." During this activity, students realized why we needed to have guidelines/rules to protect our rights as individuals and as a class. We talked about our right to learn and what behaviors interrupted that right. Students shared how one interruption to their learning was feeling bad when they didn't know something, especially when someone pointed it out. Students agreed that, "It's OK not to know and it's OK to help someone when you do" and combined this thought with our one-word rule: Respect. This resulted in us using the phrase, "respectfully disagree" whenever correcting someone in our classroom.

Experiences that Encourage Change and Growth. Classrooms should be safe places for our students to make mistakes and learn. Giving students feedback and opportunities for revision before assigning a lasting grade encourages them to continue growing. If we know that making errors will help learning, then learning experiences must provide opportunities for the learner to struggle. This productive struggle, or cognitive conflict, helps the brain muscle grow more than any fail-safe lesson plans can.

After learning from mistakes, it is then important to help the learner move on. This encourages the learner to have a mindset to try again. Carol Dweck, author of *Mindset: The New Psychology of Success,* (2016) compares a fixed mindset that focuses on a specific outcome with a growth mindset that finds value in the process of learning. Schools serve students best when there is a growth mindset culture in which continuous learning is the focus.

Some of my best learning experiences about growth mindset happened while working at the Boys and Girls Club. This difference-making organization has a mission to "to enable all young people, especially those who need us most, to reach their full potential as productive, caring, responsible citizens" (Boys and Girls Club - Our Mission & Story., n.d.). In addition to offering a variety of opportunities for kids to be able to play, interact, and learn together, the Boys and Girls Club philosophy reminds them daily that they belong and have something valuable to share. The caring feedback that staff members would give to kids who were displaying destructive or inappropriate behavior had three parts. First, there was a corrective action to ensure safety and to stop the behavior. Second, there was a conversation reminding the child that they belonged, they were a club member, and this space would be protected for them in the same way that it was being protected for others. Kids had the opportunity to explain why the behavior happened and could provide input as to a resolution. Finally, depending on the situation, they would be asked to go home for the day or activate the resolution that was agreed upon. The staff member would remind them that tomorrow was a new day, that they would be welcomed back to the Club with a clean slate, and that it was up to them to keep it that way.

When a learner feels stuck, they might be unable to communicate their thinking. This is when a teacher can encourage and help them answer the following questions: What actions or resources are required immediately in order to correct this mistake? What can I control about the situation? Who can I collaborate or connect with that has found success in this learning experience? We help learners grow from their mistakes when they are involved in the study of what has worked and hasn't worked in their learning.

We help learners grow from their mistakes when they are involved in the study of what has worked and hasn't worked in their learning.

Responsive and Actionable Feedback

Teachers are positioned to coach and mentor their students as they work through learning experiences. Feedback that is given can either support or stunt growth depending on intent and timeliness. When giving feedback it is important to know that the brain remembers more of the negative than the positive. Criticism or uninvited feedback can be harmful and can cause the learner to go backwards in their learning. Learners are more likely to invite feedback that encourages an action, offers choice, and comes from a person who they respect and look up to. While students are experiencing both successes and failures, teachers can be matchmakers between needs that arise with resources that are available. One way that teachers can encourage students to reflect and communicate about their learning is by empowering them to be key communicators between school and home. Help learners find ways to share their successes and mistakes with their families. Celebrate both the peaks and the valleys, as both are part of any learning journey.

While students are experiencing both successes and failures, teachers can be matchmakers between needs that arise with resources that are available.

Experiences that Identify Learning Barriers and Encourage Continuous Learning. Feedback is both responsive and actionable, when two-way communication is happening between the teacher and the student. This can look like the teacher providing explicit instruction to support a learning goal, and the learner explaining what they know and what they don't know. Then, together, the teacher and student co-design experiences that will give needed instruction and remove any learning barrier to help keep the student moving forward toward their learning goal.

I'm grateful for many caring and wise teachers who have provided me with responsive and actionable feedback to encourage my learning growth. Doug Park, president of *Systems for World Class Competitiveness* is one such person. Park shared a treasure that he adapted from Chris Argyis' (2008) work on double-loop learning that he refers to as Triple Loop Learning. It connects to a Learn-Do-Earn cycle and encourages continuous learning for both employees and employers. Argyis (2008) explains that Double-Loop Learning is a process encouraging people to keep learning by thinking about their own assumptions and beliefs and determining what new information or skills are needed to solve problems. The following visual is based on both of these ideas and offers suggestions for how teachers can provide responsive and actionable feedback to the learners they serve. The table below integrates this concept with our *Oath for Learners* and shows how to activate feedback through two-way communication between teacher and student to continue learning.

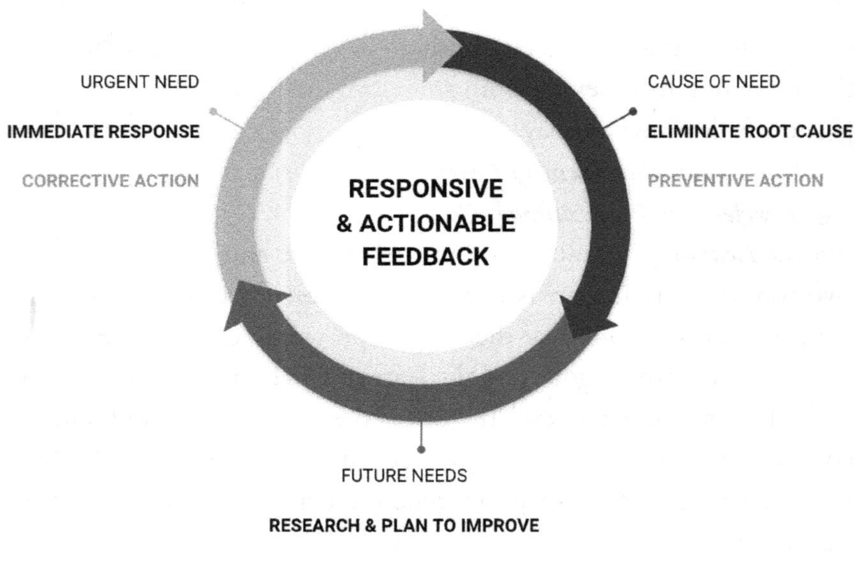

1st Response - LISTEN & EMPOWER	2nd Response - ANALYZE & RESOURCES	3rd Response - EXPERIENCES & RELATIONSHIPS
URGENT **NEED** Why is my learning goal valuable?	CAUSE OF **NEED** Revisit what is interrupting my learning for this goal.	FUTURE **NEED** Reflect on what skills and knowledge gained through the learning goal. Is more practice or research needed for continued growth?
IMMEDIATE RESPONSE What is interrupting my learning?	ELIMINATE ROOT CAUSE What instruction or support is needed to remove the learning barrier(s)?	A PLAN TO IMPROVE What would have made this learning experience better?
CORRECTIVE ACTION Teacher and student co-design a learning plan connecting student's strengths and interests for next steps.	**PREVENTIVE ACTION** Teacher and student revise the learning plan in response to the cause of need, removing barrier(s), and providing necessary resources for next steps.	**REFLECTIVE ACTION** What more is needed to master the learning goal? Or if mastered, how will the skills/knowledge serve a need for the learner or their community?

Responsive and actionable feedback keeps learners thinking and gives them space and time to practice and revise until mastering a skill or a concept, ultimately helping each student develop their full potential. Here's a classroom example, where responsive and actionable feedback helped a learner begin writing with hopes for developing within the student a future desire to communicate using written and verbal skills:

Derek would tell stories that were imaginative and detailed; however, when an activity required writing, he would freeze. There was an assumption that by the grade level that Derek was in, he would have already developed an understanding of how letters make words, words can make phrases, phrases can make complete sentences, and complete sentences can be put together to form paragraphs. In my experience, I noticed students who struggled with spelling and punctuation would avoid writing. Derek did struggle with spelling words and using punctuation correctly, but this wasn't the root of the problem. He hadn't found success in writing in the past because there were too many moving parts. Derek had complex ideas in his mind that didn't look right to him when he tried to put them on paper. He would become frustrated with a few simple sentences that he had crafted because they didn't reflect the thoughts that he had in his mind. Writing was letting him down; therefore, he didn't want to give writing any of his time.

Experiences That Connect Interests to Learning Goals. When learners are not motivated to try, it's helpful to find something that a student is interested in or good at and connect this to the learning goal. Derek loved an animated series on YouTube that featured a silly and sometimes crude piece of fruit. I found an app on my phone that allowed you to make animated fruit videos, where the eyes and lips were yours and the rest was a piece of fruit. Derek liked the idea of using this app. We made a plan for him to use this tool after completing at least one paragraph; he would have permission to go to my desk and use this app on my phone to create a video of what he had on paper. For extra fun, he could choose to share this video with his mom by emailing it directly to her from the app. We agreed on the plan and I expected that Derek would make progress in his writing.

The next time I presented a writing activity to the class, I looked at Derek, expecting him to be engaged, but instead his head was down and he was visibly agitated. I walked over to Derek's table and sat next to him, and quietly reminded him "This is your opportunity to create your own video and send it to your mom." His eyes smiled a little, but then quickly turned to disappointment. "I can't," he replied, "my words are stuck in my head."

I asked him to tell me about what he was thinking and he shared a story that would easily fill a page or two. "Maybe we could use the app in a different way, Derek. What if you recorded this story first, just like you told it to me? Then we can work on getting it from the video to your paper?" This did it! The process that Derek needed was to narrate his own thoughts in a recording of some kind and then listen to them played back for him. He was able to successfully dictate what he heard, which was his original work. Derek found a successful process for writing through responsive and actionable feedback that connected to his interests and strengths.

1st Response - LISTEN & EMPOWER	2nd Response - ANALYZE & RE-SOURCES	3rd Response - EXPERIENCES & RELATIONSHIPS
Urgent Need The student refused to write.	Cause of Need The student wanted to write his stories exactly as he thought them, and hadn't found independent success.	Future Need What experiences can be available to help the student be successful in future writing goals?
Immediate Response Teacher talked to the student and discovered that he could communicate his thoughts well during speaking.	Eliminate Root Cause Although the student could craft stories in his mind, he struggled to get complex ideas from his mind onto paper.	Research and Plan What instructional support could help with processing speed, sequencing, and language skills?
Corrective Action Teacher and student created a learning plan that connected the student's interest to the writing goal.	Preventive Action The teacher activated the student's strength, along with technology resources to help the student have a will and a way to reach the writing goal.	Reflective Action Experiences that connected the student's interests along with the option to share his writing projects with his mom, helped the student continue to develop his writing skills.

Experiences That Last. Providing responsive and actionable feedback takes time. It is hard work and sometimes impossible to do alone because of the workload a teacher has. The visuals and examples above have been shared to support your thinking about what responsive and actionable feedback can look like for you, your students, and anyone on your support team. Your effort matters and makes a lasting impact throughout a person's life. I like to imagine Derek in the workplace, just flowing with his writing skills; perhaps the time and effort that I shared with him has influenced some of this.

How do students naturally share responsive and actionable feedback with each other? Critical life skills can be gained from experiencing learning with peers, and this is one of the key reasons why students want to come to school. Learners of all ages enjoy learning with friends. Kindergarteners share experiences that encourage learning how to regulate emotions and behaviors, take turns, and advocate for their needs. Elementary students develop the ability to see multiple perspectives along with learning how to manage conflict. Teenagers challenge each other in the areas of social support and setting boundaries. Adults find ways to learn together and support each other in whatever stage of life that they are in from young adults to grandparents.

Connections and Innovation

Activating the *Oath for Learners* helps teachers set up valuable connections and opportunities for innovation to take place. Creating lesson plans or learning experiences for students shifts from a script or a guess at reaching the target to customized offerings that have been developed with input from students. Take another look at the *Oath for Learners* and review the valuable prep work that is done prior to creating the learning experiences for students.

An *Oath for Learners*

As a teacher, I pledge to **listen** to and **empower** my students to develop their full potential. I will **analyze** and study my students. I will help provide hope to my students by matching **resources** to their **needs** and providing **experiences** that support each student's growth. I will model the power of a team and help my students build lasting **relationships.** Ultimately, I realize that to help a learner, I need to be a learner myself.

In addition to keeping the *Oath for Learners* in motion, teachers can collaborate with families, employers, and study current events to determine what learning outcomes will help students the most. Some common themes that are discussed in education and the workplace include the following desired learning outcomes for students:

Emotional Intelligence
Creativity and Innovation
Adaptability
Data Literacy
Digital Literacy
Procedural Learning
Recalling and storing critical information

This list, along with the expected standards and use of required curriculum, can become overwhelming. I remember the hours I spent trying to wrap my head around where to start with my students, while looking over pacing guides, curriculum maps, and standards documents. The heavy lift began to lighten as I started integrating technology, connecting with other educators, and ultimately involving my students in the creation of their learning experiences.

My students and I struck gold when we discovered that connecting with other schools from around the globe was a possibility. It all began with the question, "What can we do with five iPads?" We were so excited to put these tools to use. While attending the *Discovery Education Network Summer Institute*, I met an innovative teacher from Canada and she introduced me to her son, an international teacher in Indonesia. Together, we decided to start a virtual book club, calling it *Read Across Borders*. We chose five different books and added dates to the calendar to provide real-time experiences for our students to connect through video conferencing. The goal was to have students read together and share in conversations about their reading. We connected weekly with our Canadian friends and with our friends in Indonesia using pre-recorded videos, due to our different time zones.

There was one real-time video opportunity with our friends in Indonesia because they were on a field trip and staying together in a hostel overnight. We shared a video conference with them right before they went to bed, and right after we arrived at school in the morning. This opened up deeper discoveries about time zones and why we have them. On this particular day, all my students wore hats to participate in our school's themed event. Our friends in Indonesia wanted to see each of the hats, so we made an impromptu parade giving each student a chance to walk by the iPad camera. There was a scream of delight when my student wearing a SpongeBob hat noticed that a student in Indonesia was wearing a SpongeBob pajama shirt. My student said, "We are not that different; we both like SpongeBob!"

Our class continued to explore ways to connect globally through *Mystery Skype* events that helped us use critical thinking and geography skills. We also participated in *Rock Our World*, where we collaborated with countries from all over the world to create a song using Apple's *GarageBand*. Parents joined in the fun during our *Rock Our World* global outreach event, where each school team shared their part of the song from their location.

Our global connections expanded to a universal outreach through Commander Chris Hadfield who shared his experience at the

International Space Station through Twitter and YouTube, giving my students and me our first virtual learning experience in Outer Space.

From the International Space Station kitchen, Commander Hadfield shared the steps that he took when making a peanut butter and jelly sandwich. After watching this video, we took turns creating PB & J sandwiches in small groups. Students were surprised to find that while we had mostly the same ingredients (due to allergies, a few students had other ingredients), there were a variety of ways to build a sandwich. Learning experiences such as these include content, processes, and tools that can be customized or personalized according to need or preference.

Unpacking Our Peanut Butter and Jelly Learning Experience

Content - The ingredients or content of a sandwich, can be modified according to allergies or preference.

Processes - How you make the sandwich varies according to the way that this has been modeled for you or what makes the most sense to you. The process for making a PB & J with gravity is different than without gravity.

Tools - The tools that you use for making a sandwich can be based on preference or what you have available. A butter knife, fingers, or spoon can be great tools for sandwich making. If you are making a sandwich at the International Space Station, then a squeeze tube container will most likely be required.

Presentation - How you display your sandwich, prior to eating it, can be out of necessity or preference. Some students preferred keeping the sandwich whole, others cut theirs in half or removed the crusts. Some students felt that serving a PB & J with a glass of milk was a necessity.

Outcome - An edible sandwich was the same outcome no matter the types of ingredients, how it was created, or the venue in which it was created.

If we measured the success of this PB & J learning experience as a process to build skills, rather than just the outcome of an edible sandwich (a product), it could look like this:

Emotional Intelligence - Students used self-regulation, self-awareness, and social skills to share the tools while making the sandwiches.

Creativity and Innovation - Students created a sandwich according to their preference and needs. While some sandwiches were similar, no two sandwiches were exactly the same.

Adaptability - Students who had allergies needed to use other ingredients, and some might have needed to have a separate space for building their sandwich.

Data Literacy - We could have collected data about the different ways that students presented their sandwiches. How many preferred a whole sandwich compared to a sandwich that was cut in pieces?

Digital Literacy - We used social media and YouTube to connect with Commander Chris Hadfield. This added additional information for us to think about, such as the effect of gravity.

Procedural Learning - Students thought about how they've watched a sandwich being made before. They either adopted that process or created their own.

Recalling or Storing Critical Information - Students used a proper handwashing technique and followed a safety protocol when using the butter knives.

Reflection is what makes the learning stick, so having students think back to how the activity connects to a series of skills or goals can become the most valuable part of the learning experience. While students are reflecting on the experience, teachers can be listening to their interests and looking for potential extensions or segues into the next learning experience.

My students were so enthralled from the PB & J lesson that Commander Hadfield shared with us, that they searched for more information from him. Some of my students viewed more of his videos and could explain why you can't cry in outer space, along with tips on sleeping in space. It's a great idea to run with the students when they are captivated by the learning and then look for ways to develop the required standards/skills within this. While students bring the wonder and play, teachers can help with connections.

Children are natural innovators, using their imagination to create solutions to problems or jobs that need to get done. A special memory comes to mind of a shopping trip, where my granddaughter and I were out looking for a special toy. As we walked the toy aisles, she discovered a problem. She wanted more than one toy. I reminded her about our budget for the toy and explained that she could maybe find two toys, but they would have to stay within the amount of money that we had to spend. We continued to walk for a bit, and she stopped, looked up and asked, "Grammy, do you have paper at your house?" I let her know that we did have paper. Then she said, "Well, let's just go, we can make everything that we need with paper." My granddaughter demonstrated confidence in her ability to innovate and create her own toys. Her parents nurtured her sense of wonder and even as a young learner, she knew how to use scissors, tape, and fold paper.

Harvard Professor and thought leader on innovation, Clayton Christenson, shared a presentation, "Where Does Growth Come From?" during *Talks at Google* (August 2016) explaining, "Every day jobs arise in our lives and when jobs arise, we need to find a way to get these jobs done." My granddaughter felt that the job to get done was to create all the toys that she wanted to take home from the store. In fact, we didn't buy a single toy that day because her mind was already working on how she would make all that she needed out of paper.

Innovators are out to solve a problem, sometimes using a new creation and other times with a mashup of existing creations. Innovation is about exploring possibilities; it can be messy, and it can be easy to miss. Before I made this connection, I provided feedback to my students on the product that would "Wow" me the most, rather than looking deeper at the thinking, action, or process that the student was sharing. I would like to go back in time and update some of the grades that I've given students. One time in particular, my students were sharing their ideas for a Rube Goldberg machine that would have multiple steps or processes in place to accomplish a specific goal or task. Some students shared their thoughts in an animated PowerPoint, while others teamed up to create a Rube Goldberg machine using the Minecraft video game. For each presentation, the students would use a rubric to provide feedback on the presenter's concept. At the end of the day, I found a crumpled paper on the ground and for some reason before throwing it in the trash, I unfolded it. What I saw inside was a complex Rube Goldberg machine that had been sketched with pencil, erased, and re-sketched multiple times, and it was incredible. When I visited with the student who created this masterpiece the next day, he explained that he was embarrassed to share because it was just on a "messy piece of paper." This lesson about valuing the learning more than the presentation when giving feedback to learners or grading their work, has always stayed with me.

Students will be encouraged to create and innovate when they are part of the decision-making process for their learning. Students need to see the job that needs to get done and then determine if they are interested in doing this and how they might go about it. Students also need to see that the lessons or experiences connect to a need or desired purpose. Learners should have a seat at the innovation table, with their teachers giving them the opportunity to be involved in the research and creation of these experiences. When teachers are sharing this part of their job with their learners, it frees up time for them to provide responsive and actionable feedback while the learning is in process.

Activate EXPERIENCES for Learners

This chapter unpacked Plato's quote, "Human Behavior flows from three main sources: desire, emotion, and knowledge," and connected it with three key features: allowing for the Oops!, providing Responsive and Actionable Feedback, and engaging students in Connections and Innovation, to answer the question, "What is Valuable to Learners?" Learners will find experiences valuable when they understand the purpose for learning, realize that they are supported, and know that they have an important part to play in the learning opportunities.

Oops!
Think through the following questions and then take on a challenge or two below.

- How are mistakes viewed and cared for in your classroom?
- What strategies, processes, and resources do you use to show that failure is a part of the learning process?
- In what ways are successes and failures celebrated?

Oops! Challenges:

- Share an epic failure with your students. Talk about the learning that happened, along with your wishes of how this could have gone differently.

- Provide students with a key phrase to use when they make a mistake. Toddlers know the word, "Uh-Oh" and use this when a spill or accident happens. The next step after recognition of the mistake is to take action to resolve it. For example, grab a paper towel or pick up the cup that has fallen over. Talk to your students about how they have resolved a mistake in the past.

- With your students, brainstorm mistakes that could cause harm and why rules and procedures could be in place to avoid danger. There are some mistakes that even if they taught you a valuable lesson, could leave a lasting scar or problem.

Responsive and Actionable Feedback:
Using the responsive and actionable feedback visual or table in this chapter, unpack one of your most recent learning experiences, where you moved past a struggle or a failure. Did you receive responsive and actionable feedback that encouraged you to try again or grow?

- Talk with your colleagues about how they provide feedback to their students. Is there a process in place that allows for teachers to provide more than one response and action during a learning experience? How does feedback affect the option for students to revise and edit? When reporting on the learning, such as with grades, what would be more valuable to the students continued growth?

- Reflect on a week of teaching and calculate how much time you are offering feedback. Do you offer more time to one of the following: corrective, preventive, or reflective action? What is most helpful to your students and why?

Connections and Innovation:

Invite students and their families to join you in solving problems that matter to them and that meet a need in your community. Together, look at content, processes, and tools that would be helpful when solving the selected problems or getting the needed jobs done.

Explore ways to connect with other classrooms through the *Global Read Aloud* project:

Find ways to lighten your load in the creation of learning experiences by involving your students. Ask your students how they want to update a lesson or change an experience for the better. Be available to support them, but let them drive. You will be amazed at where they will take you!

Finding the True, Good, and Beautiful

Learning experiences can provide purposeful practice by paying attention to the true, good, and beautiful that comes from the natural process of learning and involving students in their learning:

True	**Good**	**Beautiful**
Start by setting clear goals with learners, making sure that learners care about their goals.	Plan for ways to encourage and celebrate learning steps (successes and failures) on the way to achieving their goals.	Offer responsive and actionable feedback that is valuable to each learner and watch them reach their goal for a desired skill or competency.
Visualize together what success would look like, helping learners see themselves "crossing the finish line."	Help learners see how reaching their learning goals support others and themselves.	Once the learner has reached the goal, or finish line, reflect on the process, celebrate the growth, and connect to potential new learning goals.
I Know...	**So That I Can...**	**Which Helps Me...**

CHAPTER 7

Relationships: How Will I Connect with Learners?

Listen, Empower, Analyze, Resources, Needs, Experiences, ***Relationships***

"All learning is in the learner, not the teacher."
Plato

Our final step in the *Oath for Learners* has already been in action throughout the other steps. By **L**istening, **E**mpowering, **A**nalyzing, providing **R**esources for the **N**eeds of your students, you know how to connect with them and have done this in the **E**xperiences that you've offered. Learning is in the learner, as Plato explains in the above quote, and teachers encourage learners through **Relationships.** Discovering the true, good, and beautiful that come from being a person, shows us that it's all about the L.E.A.R.N.E.R.

Self-care nurtures the *true* in a person, helping them recognize their needs, their strengths, and what inspires their sense of wonder. Being a connected learner encourages the *good* in a person, through the support that they give to and receive from others. Connected learners discover who they can trust for help, along with finding out why their learning goals are valuable to them or to others. When learners create and contribute using their unique strengths, attributes, and skill sets, the results are *beautiful.* Teachers can be instrumental in helping learners know themselves and how to develop positive relationships with others. The visual below connects the *Job of the Learner* that is supported through the *Oath for Learners.*

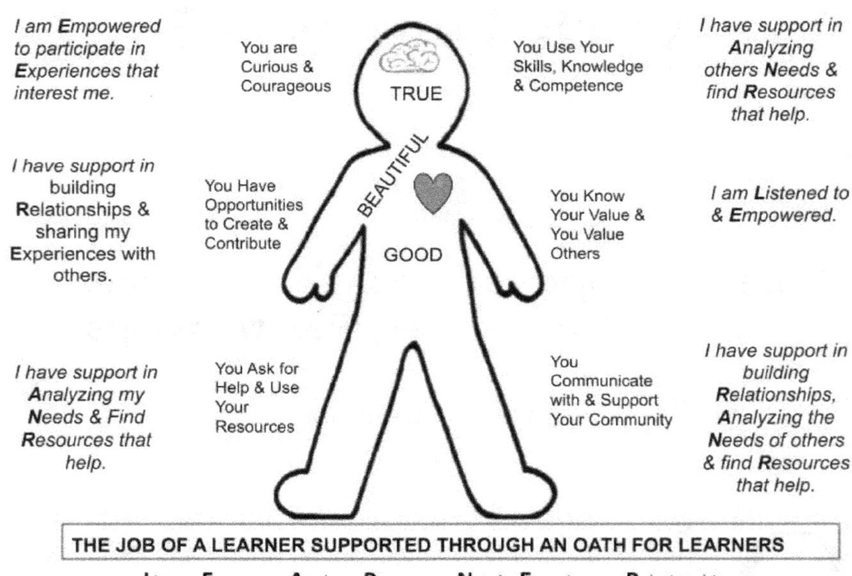

THE JOB OF A LEARNER SUPPORTED THROUGH AN OATH FOR LEARNERS

Listen, **E**mpower, **A**nalyze, **R**esources, **N**eeds, **E**xperiences, **R**elationships

Learner Self Care

When education is a service, then school will adapt to the needs of its customers: learners. Very young learners are advocates for their needs. When a baby cries, they have a need. Babies lack the language to articulate their needs, so their loved ones must be flexible in trying a variety of strategies to help them. Students, however, might need coaching or mentoring to develop the skills needed to advocate for themselves and their learning. Teachers develop mental lists or physical databases with many strategies that have worked to support their students along the way. It doesn't take long to realize that each student and situation is unique and needs to be addressed in real-time with overarching guidance, but nothing should be set in stone. Humans can change and develop faster than technology; therefore, our support needs to be directed at helping them help themselves.

Relationship between the learner's will and way for learning. Use the *Job of a Learner* as a tool to guide conversations with your students that will help show the relationship between their efforts, what existing skills and knowledge that they have to offer, and what support is needed for continued learning growth. Encourage them to read the following statements listed below and find one or more that they are doing really well. If there's one or more that they'd like to work on, support them in next steps. Let your students see you in a learner's role by modeling self-care, knowing what your strengths and challenges are, and how to be an advocate for your learning needs.

Your Job as a Learner

Listen: I want to learn because of my own curiosity or because I think it is valuable to me.

Empower: I believe in my own abilities to learn.

Analyze: I reflect on what I know, what I hope to learn, or what I've learned.

Resources: I ask for help or know where to find help.

Needs: I understand how I best learn and ask for help when needed.

Experiences: I learn by asking questions, collaborating, investigating, experimenting, and creating.

Relationships: I work with others to share my learning and learn from them in return.

When students are doing their job in their learning, they are not waiting for people to teach them; they are self-discovering and solving problems that are meaningful to them. When students are doing their job in their learning, they are looking for connections to see how the learning experience is worth their time. When learning is presented and cared for as a process, rather than an achievement or a product, students will be more open to trust the help offered and seek assistance when needed.

The *Job of a Learner* provides a general framework of expectations; next comes collaboration between students and teachers to create a learning plan with a place for specific goals and an area where they can check-in with each other. Finally, a learning portfolio makes learning success transparent. In short, the learner knows their job, has a plan, and can define success. The teacher then supports the learner in their job, co-designs the learning plan with the student, and provides feedback to help the student reach success. If learning was a skydiving experience, there are times when the teacher and student must work closely together in the same way that beginners start with tandem skydiving. When the student doesn't have the skills, knowledge, or attributes needed to independently jump, then scaffolding is needed to ensure safety. When a student has demonstrated mastery in the needed skills, knowledge, and demonstrates necessary attributes, then the teacher will release them to participate in solo skydiving.

Relationship between a learner's resilience and support that is available to them. When learners are not willing to learn, teachers can support them in developing learning resilience by revisiting *An Oath for Learners*:

> As a teacher, I pledge to **listen** to and **empower** my students to develop their full potential. I will **analyze** and study my students. I will help provide hope to my students by matching **resources** to their **needs** and providing **experiences** that

support each student's growth. I will model the power of a team and help my students build lasting **relationships.** Ultimately, I realize that to help a learner, I need to be a learner myself.

The Oath for Learners is designed to help teachers inspire students to have a will for learning, and a way to make growth toward their learning goals. Ask students to exercise learner self-care by looking at the relationship between their actions and the support that is available to them. When students reflect on these statements by determining if they are true or false, this could reveal an unmet need. You might also ask them to circle the words that they feel are missing from the current support that is being offered:

T/F - I am Listened to and Empowered.

T/F - I am Empowered to participate in Experiences that interest me.

T/F - I have support in Analyzing my Needs and finding Resources that help.

T/F - I have support in Analyzing others' Needs and finding Resources that help.

T/F - I have support in building Relationships and sharing my Experiences with others.

T/F - I have support in building Relationships, Analyzing the Needs of others, and finding Resources that help.

Relationship between individual learning and teamwork. When a learner is demonstrating apathy or displaying what is known as a "crab mentality," this might be a cry for help. This could be an indication that a learner is experiencing or has experienced trauma and a triage process for support should be activated. Apathy means a student displays a lack of interest, enthusiasm or concern. A "crab mentality" refers to a situation when one learner tries to put others down, or exhibits frustration as a result of others' success. The idea of "crab mentality" comes from an interesting fact of nature: if you have a bucket of crabs and one of the crabs climbs its way to the top and starts to leave the bucket, the other crabs pull it back down. Even crabs seem to have a tug-of-war between individual rights and the common good. Employers need employees that can initiate their own learning and work independently along with participating in teamwork and asking for help when needed. Humans shine when connected to a community that values them and provides them a space to receive and give support.

Connected and Contributing Learners

"Look at me!" are three common words that can be heard at playgrounds and parks. Perhaps from older kids you might hear, "Check it out!" Kids of all ages enjoy games that give them a turn to be seen, valued, and appreciated. Who are these kids usually talking to when shouting these words from the top of a slide or while doing a sweet jump on their bike? Parents, family members, friends—ultimately, their loved ones. Parents are their children's most influential teachers and when a partnership exists between home and school then good things are in store for that child. Students and parents are grateful and respond in a positive way when they know that they are listened to, heard, and valued. We need each other and we must be aware of any processes and protocols that hinder relationship building.

Relationship between learners and their school community. Learners need to know that it matters if they are at school because they have something valuable to share and something relevant to learn. Our students also need to know that they are missed and that things are not quite the same when they are not with us at school, whether in-person or in our online learning spaces. School is more than a place to provide experiences that encourage wonder, play, innovation, and mastery of essential skills; it is a place to be seen, to share, and to make friends. School is also a place that should help learners discover what they are most interested in learning more about. Every learner has unique strengths and attributes that, when developed, can fill a gap or a need in society. When learners are nurtured and supported, they can develop expertise and a desire to share with others. It is impossible to be great at everything, and this is why, as learners, we need to connect with each other.

School is more than a place to provide experiences that encourage wonder, play, innovation, and mastery of essential skills; it is a place to be seen, to share, and to make friends.

Relationship between school and home. If we thought about changing the ***P*** in our PLC process from *Professional* to *Personal*, we could have *Personal* Learning Communities that included students and their families. Honoring our students' first and most impactful teachers into the learning processes that happen during school hours takes effort, but it's good work well worth doing. Those invited to the table to problem solve and create learning plans should be the ones closest to the work; therefore, a school team would do well to plan with parents and students.

Another way to involve families, is to be a bridge builder between needs of the school and skill sets that family members possess. People like to share their expertise and experiences. The more specific we are when asking a family member to contribute to a need at school, the more likely authentic volunteering will occur. Create a list of activities that parents can choose to be involved in that would take only an hour a week, an hour a month, or a couple of times in a school year.

Having seasonal activities that can be scheduled in advance can also be helpful for families who have busy schedules. If you have an existing school activity that draws many families, look at the characteristics and the overall experience to find clues for family and community engagement. At a school where I taught, we hosted *Free Family Fun Nights* with educational games in which all members of the family could be involved. Many of the students in our school had younger siblings at home, so having volunteer activities where parents could bring their little ones made a difference in our volunteer numbers. When our family outreach events connected to the interests in the community—including local businesses—we would have great participation as well. The doorways of our schools should require the most maintenance because they are used by many in the community, making the school a hub for learning.

Students need school to be recognizable to the life that they live outside of school hours. What do your students and their families value? A school culture begins with understanding who will be coming to learn there and being responsive to them. Think about this like planning a party. The host of a party aims to make the experience appropriate, meaningful, and fun for their guests. Careful consideration has been taken for what food and beverages will be served, along with what activities will be available to enjoy. Guests are invited and are given some information about the what, when, and where the party will happen. Some invitations include suggestions about what to wear and what to bring, along with a hint about the activities that they can look forward to. How can schools provide invitations for learning, as part of an onboarding or welcoming for each student and their family? Now imagine the guest showing up for the party and think about a greeting that might occur. "Hi! It's great to see you! I'm glad you could make it; may I take your coat?" How a learner is greeted when they arrive at school sets the tone for the entire day. Students and their families need to know it matters that they are there, and sometimes all this takes is a smile.

Relationship between instruction and learning goals. Students need to know that the work they do at school matters, too. How does it feel when you are struggling to learn something new and your teacher says, "This is going to be good for you in the future."? As a teacher, I admire Mr. Miyagi's methods for teaching karate skills to Daniel in *The Karate Kid* series. The activities were set up as a progression to help Daniel develop muscle memory for the basics. As a mentor, Mr. Miyagi studied Daniel, his strengths, attributes, and weaknesses, and crafted a master plan to help him grow. However, do you remember the frustration that Daniel had when he was given the instruction to move his right hand to apply wax to a car, and his left hand to remove the wax from the car. Daniel didn't make the connection between waxing a car and learning Karate. He was expected to follow the single command, "Wax on, Wax off," and did this for hours without knowing why this was important. There's no doubt that he developed discipline and perseverance through the exercises that his teacher shared with him. You may remember the joy on Daniel's face after he realized how all the parts fit together and that he actually knew karate? His "Aha" came after confronting Mr. Miyagi with great frustration and stating that he didn't want to do the work anymore. If you haven't watched *The Karate Kid*, I'm hoping that you can glean from this story that we don't need to keep the reasons for the activities that we share with students a secret. We should connect with students in the process of developing their learning plans and give them opportunities to contribute. Students need to understand why they are learning, and it is respectful to share

Students need to understand why they are learning, and it is respectful to share this information with them.

this information with them. Teachers who invite students into the lesson-planning process realize that this enriches the overall learning process. It is also a timesaver and, ultimately, is great fun.

Relationship between use of technology and connecting with others. Technology has provided additional ways to connect with our students, families, and communities. The most recent COVID-19 events has activated more technology between home and school than ever before with video conferences, access to information, shared documents, and recorded lessons for students to participate in. Internet companies have worked to connect even the most rural communities in some way, helping families get online access for school and work purposes. We've come a long way in a short time by finding some common processes and providing connectivity.

I remember when YouTube was new and how it became important to my students. I would hear them tell each other about the videos that they were planning on making. I listened in to learn that they were making videos on how to do things, such as a cartwheel, beating a level on a video game, or sharing a dance that they had choreographed. Some of my students had parent or adult guidance involved and some did not. As this was in the early days of YouTube, I wondered: Who was watching these videos?

I found out that YouTube was kind of like a "Show and Tell" online space and kids of all ages were making content to share. One video that stood out was produced by a young learner who wanted to learn how to use a Bow drill Set, a hand-operating tool that uses friction to start a fire. This ancient technique is used in outdoor survival situations, when matches or other forms of starting a fire are not available. The camera only showed him from the kneecap down, as he held the piece of wood between his two bare feet and attempted to roll the other part with his hands. I guessed that he was seven or eight years old from the sound of his voice and his use of vocabulary. He explained that he knew that he was doing this wrong and asked YouTube viewers for help. He asked viewers to write in the comments below to help him find out what he was doing wrong. My mind was blown, first by thinking that this young kid was trying to start a fire outside by himself, without appearing to have adult supervision. Then I was fascinated that he thought of "the world" (or at least anyone watching on YouTube) as his teacher to help with a skill that he really wanted to learn. He was showing what he knew about the steps and clearly expecting that people would comment to help him. Was independent learning happening? Yes. Did the learner demonstrate perseverance? Yes. Was there evidence of problem solving and use of resources? Yes and yes! "Please tell me how to do this. Comment down below and let me know what I'm doing wrong," are the words that piqued my curiosity for how I might incorporate YouTube in my class.

The next day I tried to access YouTube at school to find that it was blocked. I guess that made sense since there is so much on YouTube that isn't appropriate for school. But when else would students learn how to navigate YouTube for academic purposes? I asked my students to raise their hand if they had watched YouTube before and every student raised their hands. Then I asked how many had made a video for YouTube, and more than half of my class raised their hands. I asked one more question, "Do your parents know that you are watching YouTube and making videos?" This time, only two students replied affirmatively. When the Internet first became accessible in our homes, many of our students were exploring and contributing there alone. Something was drawing learners of all ages to this online space. While a few might have been interested in becoming famous, most YouTube contributors wanted to connect with others to share what they had learned or receive help. The popularity of YouTube is evidence that students of all ages hope for a community to learn with and from.

Now more than ever before learners are connecting in online spaces, with YouTube being one of many places where people go for instruction, entertainment, and to curate their learning. We are digital citizens sharing resources from all over the planet. We can make global connections 24/7 and at the touch of our fingertips. As technology has become mobile, accessible, and necessary, our learners have become connected. Even at a young age, our students come to school with information overload.

Relationship between background knowledge and learning goal. Before adding new information, we can help students unpack what that they already know about a particular topic or skill. The KWL (Know, Want to know, Learn) strategy is one that we could use to honor what students are already bringing with them. Here's the strategy in a nutshell: Start with three columns on a piece of paper or digital document. One column is labeled "K" and this is a place for learners to write down everything that they already "Know" about the topic or skill. The next column is labeled "W" for students to write what they "Want" to learn. To make this especially productive, ask learners to complete this column after showing them a preview of what is to be learned. The final column labeled "L" stands for "Learn" and is a place for students to reflect on their learning. This is one strategy that can help students curate their learning and it is where formative assessment can become summative, giving teachers evidence of the learner's understanding.

Part of sorting the information is helping learners determine what is true and false. I had the opportunity to hear Alan November present at a conference during which he reflected on his experience with doctoral students who needed to learn the difference between authentic information online and fake news. November's work (2009) inspired me to improve my own "web literacy" through his resources that help learners learn how to read a web address, how to find a publisher of a website, and how to conduct advanced searches. Students of all ages need help in developing their digital citizenship and this means that schools need to incorporate the use of technology in order to be of assistance. Being in a virtual learning environment, such as a social media space or collaborating together on a live Google document, is just as real as having a conversation or working on chart paper in-person. Humans are there connecting and learning together.

Relationship between content, processes, and tools. Students need to make connections in their learning from lesson to lesson. Like many teachers, the first days of school in my classroom were always dedicated to getting to know the students. Activities included those that helped us learn about our strengths and interests. I would ask specifically about what they felt they were good at and what challenged them in different subject areas. It was common for my fifth graders to say, "I'm really good at multiplication, but not division." Or when I taught third grade, students would explain how they were great at addition, but not subtraction. This showed the number sense disconnect that students had; they didn't see the connections and it gave me an awesome place to start. Students need to see the whole picture and the parts of a story in order to develop an understanding that allows them to apply and transfer their knowledge and skills.

Helping learners see the relationship between the content, processes, and tools is a vital part of the learning process. This goes for learners of all ages and experiences. I remember facilitating some teacher professional development, where the objective was to introduce the features of Google Drive to a group of teachers. Before I started, I asked the teachers if they had any questions or goals that they wanted to accomplish during our session. One teacher asked with frustration in her voice, "Why do I need to have Google Drive, when I already have *Think Through Math*?" Then others added the many other subscriptions and online resources that they already had. This helped me know where to start. We wrote down all the tools that had recently been introduced to them and together we sorted for purpose and for time, place, and manner of using these tools. We connected these new tools with familiar workflows and soon there were smiles and teachers were exploring and planning for next steps.

Students need to see the connection between what they are learning and the way that they are being graded or assessed to show that they've learned. Are students afraid to learn? The way that we measure learning success for students can either encourage or discourage learning. Measurements or assessments of learning should be relevant, with achievable targets, and with support available.

Students need to have the opportunity to truly learn and master the essential skills that are important to them. This kind of mastery requires a school system to be flexible and to know where a student is in their learning and where their interests lie. In Sal Khan's TED Talk (2017), *Let's Teach for Mastery, Not Test Scores*, he challenges us to think about mastery and mindset to ensure that learning happens by giving students agency over their learning and allowing time to be flexible with the expectation that mastery will happen given appropriate support for the learner.

Activate RELATIONSHIPS for Learners

This chapter took us on a visit of learning through the eyes of learners to answer the question, "How will we connect with learners?" By helping students connect their *will* to learn with a *way* for a learning goal that matters to them to be accomplished. Students need help sorting all the information, much like our earlier garage cleaning analogy:

- *Keep:* What information should I hold onto, because it is valuable and viable in helping me achieve my learning goal?
- *Review/Research:* What information am I not sure about and need to research for its validity or value to my learning goal?
- *Trash:* What information should I delete or get rid of, as it is not serving me in my effort to reach my learning goal?

The more we connect with our students' families and communities, the more they will have the opportunity to see what great teachers have always seen: the learner. As educators dedicate time to developing relationships with those they serve, this helps develop school systems to be authentic, responsive, and willing to pivot when needed.

Learner Self-Care:
Start with yourself, how are you doing with learner self-care? Are you recognizing your needs, your strengths, and taking time to care for your own sense of wonder? Chances are you have natural attributes of compassion, empathy, trustworthiness, and encouragement that help you in supporting others in their learner self-care. If you're up for a challenge, add learner self-care to your daily list of things to do. There are only so many hours in the day; how many hours do you spend serving, caring

for your basic needs, and caring for your own learning? If you're feeling crabby or wishing that you had more empathy to share, you might need some additional support. Visit with a trusted friend or mentor and take some time to fill up and recover as needed.

Helping Students with Learner Self-Care

- How do we help learners identify their strengths and weaknesses?
- If you have an existing Advisory or Mentoring program at your school, how are these addressing learner self-care, in addition to other social and emotional needs?
- When learners are showing evidence of trauma or need additional support that you are not an expert to provide, what is your "triage process" for ensuring they receive the help they need?

Connected and Contributing Learners

Try a daily reflective practice of asking these questions to see how you're doing as a Connected and Contributing Learner, encouraging your students to do the same. Much like the reflective activity of noting your High Moments and Low Moments of the day, this helps learners see the relationship between their efforts and their productivity:

1. Have I learned something today? (True)
2. Did I help someone today? (Good)
3. Was I able to use my talents and skills to contribute? (Beautiful)

Activities for school or district leadership to work on with teachers, students, families, and community members:

- Reflect on an *Oath for Learners* and the *Job of the Learning* to determine current success and any barriers that could hinder either of these efforts.

An *Oath for Learners*

As a teacher, I pledge to **listen** to and **empower** my students to develop their full potential. I will **analyze** and study my students. I will help provide hope to my students by matching **resources** to their **needs** and providing **experiences** that support each student's growth. I will model the power of a team and help my students build lasting **relationships.** Ultimately, I realize that to help a learner, I need to be a learner myself.

Your Job as a Learner

Listen: I want to learn because of my own curiosity or because I think it is valuable to me.
Empower: I believe in my own abilities to learn.
Analyze: I reflect on what I know, what I hope to learn, or what I've learned.
Resources: I ask for help or know where to find help.
Needs: I understand how I best learn and ask for help when needed.
Experiences: I learn by asking questions, collaborating, investigating, experimenting, and creating.
Relationships: I work with others to share my learning or learn from them.

- **Decision-Making & Organizational Structure** - Review decision-making processes to check on how data collection and analysis include student and community input, along with reviewing organizational structures to ensure that resources are effectively used to meet the educational needs of all students.
- **Building Relationships & Learning Opportunities** - Review how your team activates collaboration within a greater learning network, including building relationships with students and parents to share in the district and school mission, vision, values, and goals, while offering ongoing learning opportunities.

Finding the True, Good, and Beautiful

If there are processes or procedures that are interrupting the opportunity for students to grow and learn, then these should be re-evaluated to see if they need to be updated, removed, or replaced. If you could wave a magic wand, what would you change in education to ensure that learners were able to connect and contribute using their unique strengths and attributes? Here are my three wishes:

Wish #1 - The "True," being what we want students to know and be able to do throughout their K-12 education, would be evaluated by local, state, national, and international communities, with family and student input to ensure that standards are truly essential competencies that learners can build on throughout their lives. We have technology that would allow us to collaborate and update these in real-time.

Wish #2 - The "Good," referring to how we connect with learners, their families, and the community, would be assessed to ensure that K-12 education is relevant and valuable in supporting students to be contributing citizens now and in their future. This connection would remove the need to refer to "real world" connections or experiences, because our schools would already serve as a vital and functional part of the "real world" in which we all exist on a daily basis.

Wish #3 - The "Beautiful," where new measures of success include an opportunity for students to share their learning success through the problems they want to solve, projects they create, and relationships they build, would be as—or more—important than more standardized ways we measure success. When we measure the success of our students, teachers, and administrators, it's important that we have attainable targets and that we do not hold people accountable to standards that are not serving them.

Teachers are Difference Makers

When someone asks what you do for a living, what is your answer? This is a great opportunity to share why you became an educator. Teachers help students learn. A person can be a teacher to another person, even without the title. Some teachers who have impacted my life taught in the classroom; others were bus drivers, coaches, friends, family members, neighbors, or complete strangers. I'll always remember being checked on by a difference maker who served lunch at my high school. When she would see me coming close, she would share a big smile and greet me by name. On many days, she was the only teacher who asked me how my day was going. Looking back on this, I think that she made the choice to greet all students by name. It was her gift to us all, whether she realized this or not. I was guaranteed to be welcomed every time that I saw her. Teaching is a sacred and timeless profession that seeks to make a difference in the lives of others.

Impactful teachers are learners and they realize that the subject they are truly studying are the people they are serving, not the content they are teaching. Knowing our students helps us view the learning experience through their eyes and gives us the necessary perspective to craft school in response to them. Educators make the biggest impact when sharing their own learning experiences. Do your students know your interests and what makes you smile? Taking time to listen to each other helps to match learning targets with learner interests, while building relationships that will allow a teacher to authentically mentor students.

Teachers are instrumental in developing home and community partnerships. Providing opportunities for students to connect and learn with the community inside and outside the school building is a step in preparing them to be contributing citizens. Allowing students to have choice in their learning increases ownership and engagement and builds skills and knowledge through their inquiry. We all have a part to play in developing a relevant and supportive educational experience for learners.

Throughout fourteen years of classroom teaching and during my various roles to support adult learners at district, state, and university learning venues, I've experienced differing views about the purpose of education. While there is agreement about who we serve, each community has a unique "why and what" that gives them deep roots in their education efforts. A seed planted in my thinking about education started during a conversation with my pre-service teaching mentor who said, "Students learn because they are naturally curious; they come to school to build relationships." Yes, schools are learning venues where students can enhance their natural ability to learn while building friendships and partnerships with other learners. Teachers know when they are successful because it shows in their students' attitudes about learning and school. Students can't wait for school to start when they know they are valued, have choices, realize that they have something to contribute, can receive help to work on things that matter to them, and can have fun with their friends.

A Teacher is Successful when they...

Listen to and Empower each student to develop their full potential.

Analyze and study each student to find out how they best learn.

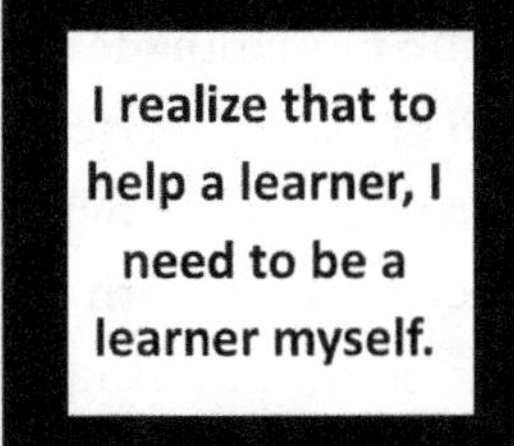

Encourage hope by matching Resources with student's Needs and provide Experiences that support each student's growth.

Model the power of a team and help students build lasting Relationships.

...and that is True, Good, and Beautiful!

If you have a job within the K-12 education system that is allowing students to learn and grow by activating their *Job as a Learner* and gives you freedom to honor an *Oath for Learners*, then you can stop reading here and celebrate. You are part of something amazing and as long as the education system that you are working in continues to be responsive and flexible, learning success will come.

If you've been reading this book, wishing for the K-12 education system that you work for or with would be responsive and flexible, keep reading. You can be a difference maker to support what you might think is impossible to become possible. As a teacher, you have treasures to share, the stories of your learners. You have had a front row seat when the learners around you have experienced an "Aha!" moment. In the same way that we need to invite learners and their families into our PLCs (Personal Learning Communities), you can share what you know will help your learners with those who are making decisions that are either supporting or inhibiting learning. Think about how you might activate your students, their families, your community, and even available technology tools to tell the incredible learner stories that you are a witness to each day. Work to get these stories of growth, success, and struggle in front of decision-makers. Tell others about barriers that are interrupting the learning process, along with ideas of how to remove these barriers. You know that communicating high expectations and finding ways to help students maximize their learning results in them developing to their full potential.

You're still reading, so I believe that we've found a problem that we are interested in solving together. Let's dream big. Let's take some beautiful risks. Share with others about what needs to be removed that is interrupting learning growth for students. Help your students share their successful learning stories. Together we can create an education service that **L**istens, **E**mpowers, **A**nalyzes, provides **R**esources, understands **N**eeds, designs **E**xperiences, and offers caring **R**elationships to support all learners.

Education as a Service to Inspire and Support Learning

An Oath to Our Learners *(What Learners Can Expect From Us)*
We will create an education service that **L**istens, **E**mpowers, **A**nalyzes, provides **R**esources, understands your **N**eeds, designs **E**xperiences, and offers caring **R**elationships.

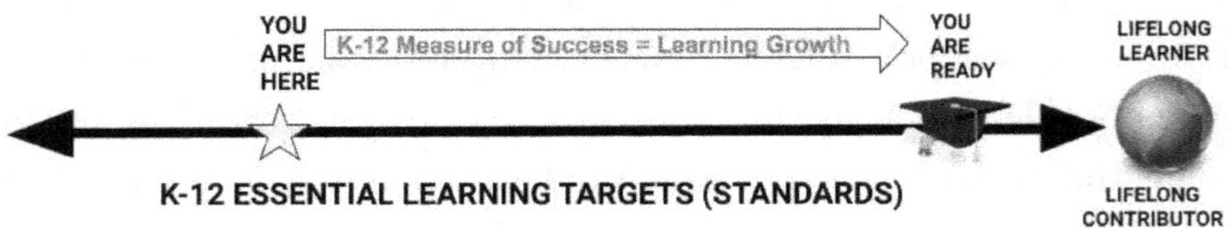

Thank you for being a difference maker in the lives of your students. Your work matters. You are not alone in your efforts to ensure that education exists as a learner-driven service that honors the True, Good, and Beautiful in every human that we serve.

References

Argyris, C. (2008). *Teaching smart people how to learn*. Boston, MA: Harvard Business Press.

Ascd. (2020). Retrieved from http://www.ascd.org/programs/The-Whole-Child/Whole-Child-Network.aspx

Beghetto,R.(2018,Dec.18).TakingBeautifulRisksinEducation.Retrievedfrom http://www.ascd.org/publications/educational-leadership/dec18/vol76/num04/Taking-Beautiful-Risks-in-Education.aspx

Bloom, B. S. (1956). Taxonomy of educational objectives: The classification of educational goals. New York: Longmans, Green.

Bloom, B.S. (1968). Learning for mastery. *Evaluation Comment (UCLA-CSEIP), 1* (2), 1–12.

Brammer, L. M., & MacDonald, G. (2003). *The helping relationship: Process and skills*. Boston: Allyn and Bacon.

Brockman, J. (1997, September 20). Truth, Beauty, and Goodness: Education for All Human Beings. Retrieved from https://stage.edge.org/conversation/howard_gardner-truth-beauty-and-goodness-education-for-all-human-beings

Boys and Girls Club - Our Mission & Story. (n.d.). Retrieved September 8, 2020, from https://www.bgca.org/about-us/our-mission-story

Burgess, D. (2018). *Teach like a pirate: Increase student engagement, boost your creativity, and transform your life as an educator*. San Diego, CA: Dave Burgess Consulting.

Casas, J. (2017). *Culturize: Every student, every day, whatever it takes.* San Diego, CA: Dave Burgess Consulting, Incorporated.

Carroll, K. (2005). *Rules of the red rubber ball: Find and sustain your life's work.* New York: ESPN Books.

Christensen, C. (2016). Where Does Growth Come From? Google Talks. Retrieved from https://www.youtube.com/watch?v=rHdS_4GsKmg

Citizenship in a Republic, *Speech at the Sorbonne, Paris, April 23, 1910 The Works of Theodore Roosevelt, Vol XIII, pp. 506-529*

Cirillo, F. (2018). *The Pomodoro Technique.* Random House UK.

Davis, A. W., & Kappler-Hewitt, K. (2013, July). Australia's Campfires, Caves. and Watering Holes. Retrieved from https://files.eric.ed.gov/fulltext/EJ1015175.pdf - ISTE Leading and Learning with Technology

Day O'Connor, J. (2009). ICivics. Retrieved from https://www.icivics.org/our-founder

Dufour, R., & Marzano, R. J. (2015). *Leaders of learning: How district, school, and classroom leaders improve student achievement.* United States: No Publisher.

Dweck, C. (2016). *Mindset the new psychology of success.* New York: Random House.

EdCamp Idaho Founders. (2014). Edcamp Idaho. Retrieved from https://sites.google.com/view/edcampidaho/home

Elbot, C. F., & Fulton, D. (2008). *Building an intentional school culture: Excellence in academics and character.* Thousand Oaks, CA: Corwin Press.

Ellis, L. (2006). *The dash: Making a difference with your life from beginning to end.* Motivate, 2012.

Ericsson, A., & Pool, R. (2017). *Peak: How all of us can achieve extraordinary things.* London: Vintage.

Fullan, M., Quinn, J., & McEachen, J. (2018). *Deep learning engage the world, change the world.* Thousand Oaks, CA: Corwin, a SAGE Company.

Guarino, K. (2019, June). The Resilience Journal: Daily Reflection & Self-Care for Educators. Retrieved from https://kami-guarino.mykajabi.com/journal

Hadfield, C. (2015). *An astronaut's guide to life on Earth*. New York: Back Bay.

Hattie, J., & Clarke, S. (2019). *Visible learning: Feedback*. London: Routledge, Taylor & Francis Group.

Heath, C., & Heath, D. (2019). *The power of moments: Why certain experiences have extraordinary impact*. London: Corgi.

Howard, R. (Director), & Grazer, B. (Producer). (1995). *Apollo 13*.

Jones, D., & Jones, S. (2020). Expeditions in Education. Retrieved from https://www.expeditionsineducation.org/

Karate Kid [Video file]. (1993). Place of publication not identified: Columbia Tristar Home Video.

Khan, S. (2017). Let's teach for mastery—not test scores. Retrieved from https://www.ted.com/talks/sal_khan_let_s_teach_for_mastery_not_test_scores

Lahey, J. (2015). *The gift of failure: How to step back and let your child succeed*. London: Short Books.

Rose, T. (2015). *End of average: The science of what makes us different*. Place of publication not identified: Harper One.

Maiers, A. (2011). You MATTER Manifesto. Retrieved from https://www.angelamaiers.com/blog/you-matter-manifesto.html

Maslow, A.H. (1943). "A Theory of Human Motivation". In *Psychological Review, 50* (4), 430-437. Washington, DC: American Psychological Association.

McTighe, J., & Willis, J. (2019). *Upgrade your teaching: Understanding by design meets neuroscience*. Alexandria, VA: ASCD.

November, A. C. (2009). Web literacy for educators. Retrieved from https://www.amazon.com/Web-Literacy-Educators-Alan-November/dp/1412958431

Oakley, B. A., Sejnowski, T. J., & McConville, A. (2018). *Learning how to learn: How to succeed in school without spending all your time studying.* New York: TarcherPerigee.

Person. (2011, April 14). Big Thinkers: Judy Willis on the Science of Learning. Retrieved from https://www.edutopia.org/video/big-thinkers-judy-willis-science-learning

Pierson, R. F. (2013). Rita F. Pierson. Retrieved from https://www.ted.com/speakers/rita_f_pierson

Pink, D. H. (2009). *Drive: The surprise truth about what motivates us.* New York: Riverhead Books.

Scherer. M. (2001, Sept.). How and Why Standards Can Improve Student Achievement: A Conversation with Robert J. Marzano. Retrieved from http://www.ascd.org/publications/educational-leadership/sept01/vol59/num01/How-and-Why-Standards-Can-Improve-Student-Achievement@-A-Conversation-with-Robert-J.-Marzano.aspx

Shareski, D. (2017). *Embracing a culture of joy.* Bloomington, IN: Solution Tree Press.

Sinek, S. (2009). *Start with why how great leaders get everyone to take action.* New York: Portfolio.

Snyder, C. R. (2010). *Psychology of Hope: You Can Get Here from There.* Riverside: Free Press.

Spencer, J., & Juliani, A. J. (2017). *Empower: What happens when students own their learning.* San Diego?: IMpress.

The Aurora Institute. (2020). *A New Dawn for Every Learner.* https://aurora-institute.org/

The Aspen Institute National Commission on Social, Emotional, and Academic Development. (2019, March 14). From a Nation at Risk to a Nation at Hope. Retrieved from http://nationathope.org/

The Good Project. (2020). Retrieved from http://www.pz.harvard.edu/projects/the-good-project

founded as "The GoodWork Project" by psychologists Mihaly Csikszentmihalyi, William Damon, and Howard Gardner in 1996.

The Imagineering Story: Disney. (2019). Retrieved from https://www.disneyplus.com/series/the-imagineering-story/6ryoXv1e1rWW

Tyson, P. (2001, March 27). The Hippocratic Oath Today. Retrieved from https://www.pbs.org/wgbh/nova/article/hippocratic-oath-today/

Vygotsky, L. S. (1978). *Mind in society: The development of higher psychological processes.* Cambridge, MA: Harvard University Press.

Wadsworth, B. J. (1971). Piaget's theory of cognitive development: An introduction for students of psychology and education. New York: McKay.

Williams, Heather P. "Horses Preparing Superintendent Candidates for the Leadership Arena." *Journal of Experiential Education*, 2020, p. 105382592096634., doi:10.1177/1053825920966340.

Willis J. (2007). The Neuroscience of Joyful Education. Retrieved from http://www.ascd.org/publications/educational-leadership/summer07/vol64/num09/The-Neuroscience-of-Joyful-Education.aspx

Willis, J. (2016, February 11). Brain Development and Adolescent Growth Spurts. Retrieved from https://www.edutopia.org/blog/brain-development-adolescent-growth-spurts-judy-willis

Yale Center for Emotional Intelligence: A Systematic Approach to SEL. (n.d.). Retrieved from https://www.ycei.org/ruler

Mood Meter

125 Common Interview Questions and Answers (With Tips). (2020). Retrieved from https://www.indeed.com/career-advice/interviewing/top-interview-questions-and-answers

About the Author

Marita Diffenbaugh has served as a teacher, administrator, and has provided leadership support for districts, schools, and classrooms. Marita gained expertise and experience as a student-focused, purpose driven servant leader and uses this to support school and district leadership in the strategic development of mastery-based education and instructional technology implementation.

Marita is currently sharing her passion and leadership skills to support the expansion of Elevate Academy, a public Career Technical charter school of choice for students in 6th-12th grades who are not finding success in their current education. As a partner with Elevate Academy's co-founders, Marita is connecting education with industry and community by developing, planning, and launching this new North Idaho school in Fall 2022.

As a connected educator, she has shared professional development with educators through local, state, national, and international presentations with a focus on the process of learning in both in-person and virtual spaces, care for learners of all ages, and encouragement for positive digital citizenship. Being a co-Founder of #EdCampIdaho, facilitator/participant of the Idaho Mastery Education Network, #IDedchat, Discovery Education Network, and iCivics has kept Marita learning with a personal learning network of dynamic educators.

As a passionate learner, Marita enjoys connecting learning goals to community resources and needs. She believes that hope is a prerequisite for learning and looks for opportunities to help others see their value. She also believes that every human being has something amazing to share with the world, and she looks for ways to help learners of all ages develop their full potential.

Marita is dedicated to using her strengths and experiences to advocate for respect and opportunity for all learners. If you are interested in booking collaborative learning sessions, contact her at maritadiffenbaugh@gmail.com. You can also connect with her on Twitter or Voxer: @MDiffenbaugh or on Instagram: MaritaDiffenbaugh

More from ConnectEDD Publishing

Since 2015, ConnectEDD has worked to transform education by empowering educators to become better-equipped to teach, learn, and lead. What started as a small company designed to provide professional learning events for educators has grown to include a variety of services to help teachers and administrators address essential challenges. ConnectEDD offers instructional and leadership coaching, professional development workshops focusing on a variety of educational topics, a roster of nationally recognized educator associates who possess hands-on knowledge and experience, educational conferences custom-designed to meet the specific needs of schools, districts, and state/national organizations, and ongoing, personalized support, both virtually and onsite. In 2020, ConnectEDD expanded to include publishing services designed to provide busy educators with books and resources consisting of practical information on a wide variety of teaching, learning, and leadership topics. Please visit us online at connecteddpublishing.com or contact us at:

info@connecteddpublishing.com

Recent Publications:

Live Your Excellence: Action Guide by Jimmy Casas

Culturize: Action Guide by Jimmy Casas

Daily Inspiration for Educators: Positive Thoughts for Every Day of the Year by Jimmy Casas

Eyes on Culture: Multiply Excellence in Your School by Emily Paschall

Pause. Breathe. Flourish.: Living Your Best Life as an Educator by William D. Parker

www.ingramcontent.com/pod-product-compliance
Lightning Source LLC
Chambersburg PA
CBHW062108040426
42336CB00042B/2586

9781734890860